W9-BNP-248

POETICALLY
Speaking
ARTISTICALLY

THELMA CUNNINGHAM

NLT

Scripture quotations marked NLT are taken from the Holy Bible, New Living Translation, copyright © 1996, 2004, 2007. Used by permission of Tyndale House Publishers, Inc. Carol Stream, Illinois 60188. All rights reserved. Website NRSV

NKJV

Scripture quotations marked NKJV are taken from the New King James Version. Copyright © 1982 by Thomas Nelson, Inc. Used by permission. All rights reserved.

KJV

Scripture quotations marked KJV are from the Holy Bible, King James Version (Authorized Version). First published in 1611. Quoted from the KJV Classic Reference Bible, Copyright © 1983 by The Zondervan Corporation.

ESV

Unless otherwise indicated, all scripture quotations are from The Holy Bible, English Standard Version® (ESV®). Copyright ©2001 by Crossway Bibles, a division of Good News Publishers. Used by permission. All rights reserved.

NIV

Scripture quotations marked NIV are taken from the Holy Bible, New International Version®. NIV®. Copyright © 1973, 1978, 1984 by International Bible Society. Used by permission of Zondervan. All rights reserved. [Biblica]

Copyright © 2017 by Thelma Cunningham. 763508

ISBN: Softcover 978-1-5434-3948-9
EBook 978-1-5434-3947-2

All rights reserved. No part of this book may be reproduced or transmitted in any form or by any means, electronic or mechanical, including photocopying, recording, or by any information storage and retrieval system, without permission in writing from the copyright owner.

Print information available on the last page.

Rev. date: 01/22/2018

To order additional copies of this book, contact:
Xlibris
1-888-795-4274
www.Xlibris.com
Orders@Xlibris.com

DEDICATED TO MY DAD
ROBERT CHAPMAN
MY MOM IN HEAVEN
THELMA CHAPMAN
ALL MY FAMILY AND FRIENDS
JESUS WHO GAVE ME
THE TALENT INSPIRATION
AND ABILITY

TABLE OF CONTENTS

LOVE POEMS

****

EVERY DAY MESSAGES

SPIRITUAL AWAKENING

SONGS SPIRITUAL
&
R & B SONGS

30.	NEW JERSAULEM	46.	SOUND OF THE SAINTS
31.	LEAVE THEM BEHIND	47.	ONE WAY WITH GOD
32.	COME FOLLOW JESUS	48.	THAT DO YOU WANNA DO
33.	HAPPIER TOMORROW	49.	NOT HOPELESS
34.	WHY ARE YOU ON YOUR WAY	50.	MAKE UP YOUR MIND
35.	JUST PUT YOUR TRUST IN HIM/ TOMORROW	51.	GOD CHANGED ME
		52.	HANGING OUT NO MORE
36.	JUSTICE SOUND	53.	WHEN YOU MAKE UP YOUR MIND
37.	TUMULTUOUS STORM	54.	I LOVE MY JESUS
38.	THERE ALL GONE	55.	IT'S ALL OVER ME
39.	I WILL DO NOTHING AT ALL	56.	NO ONE COULD TELL ME
40.	WHAT AN AMAZING GOD	57.	WHILE YOUR WAITING ON THE NEXT THING
41.	BY HIS AMAZING GRACE		
42.	CELEBRATION	58.	WHERE WERE YOU WHEN I CAME
43.	THERE IS A SAVIOR	59.	MADE IT TO THE CHURCH
44.	WHAT A WONDERFUL SAVIOR THAT WE SERVE	60.	CAN I GET A YES
		61.	I YIELD
45.	IT TAKES A MINUTE	62.	LORD YOU LIVE IN MY HEART

R & B SELECTIONS

1.	IT'S COLD OUTSIDE	5.	NOW HE IS GONE
2.	THAT SMILE	6.	THINKING ABOUT IT SONG
3.	I MISS YOU	7.	YOU SAID WHAT YOU SAID
4.	I WANT TO GIVE IT TO YOU		

Love

DO NOT PAY ATTENTION

Do not pay attention to my tears as they fall,
They must exude, disburden my despondency,
They will bechance, materialize,
Yes,
This will happen while and as my emotions ameliorate,
Wash away the chaos, hurt, and painful, memories
of you,
All,
I am going through quite an ordeal right now,
However,
Do not think that this will never end,
My tears, my sorrowing, morning of a lost lover
And friend,
Or that this sorrow which has besieged me with what
appears like an eternal continuum of feelings of
rejection,
Of just being dumbstruck, bewildered, and mystified
will never
stop, end, and simply go away,
From within me will rise inner strength, inner beauty,
Illuminating a prosperous, joyous, awe-inspiring end,
Sorrow, debility may permeate my very emotions,
mind,
And then,
They may filter through me physically,
Affecting the way I sit, or stand with a display of
weakness,
Or even at times immobilize the very utilization
of my hands,
Because,
They may be attending to tears that will falling,

All that I normally attend
May cease to function for a while,
For days,
Even weeks,
As the time passes,
Because the sorrowful, pitiful, complex ordeal
Of letting go is not easy,
You know,
I may even bewail a time or two out loud,
Or groan fretfully, and continually as my eyes turn red
while I lay on and possibly in my bed,
I may shed them, these tears, when you are not around,
But again,
Soon they will cease,
Although it may take what seems like forever or weeks,
My eyes will finally turn back with corner stones of
white,
They will again be sparkly, happy, bright,
Because the light of heaven radiating from above
Will be rejuvenating my soul from within, friend,
My heart will then be clear of the agony,
discomfort and
Fears,
The heartache of not ever seeing you again,
The hearing of your voice,
Your footsteps,
You see even these, the very sound pattern of your feet,
The not beholding a smile from your face,
The not seeing and beholding your warm, pleasant
expressions
for me filled with love, joy, patience, compassion,

And yes, even grace,
The what is the no longer the you and me,
The broken vows,
The love that ceased,
The many enduring moments shared and treasured,
held
captive in memory,
The what use to be of you and me that I will no longer
experience,
For it will again all be but a memory, memories,
They all will be in a file stored in my head,
Each and all memories no longer to sorrow about
Or fret,
And,
I will no longer be marooned in the I remember when,
Then,
One day when our love files are opened,
On display,
Those memories will have lost their ability to cause
such
sorrow, glumness, dread,
Instead,
Like fresh, falling, glistening misty rain on my green
grass,
Like the fresh, morning dew, my emotions will have
healed,
Have rejuvenated, they will revivify, they will be
renewed,
My heartache will be gone too,
And I may still sob then a time or two but the tears
May be none or maybe just a few,
Yes,
This I will go through as I get over us,

As I get over you,
Each moment that passes,
Each second that unfolds,
Will reveal a new me,
For I will no longer be an infantile,
Or puerile, unsophisticated at love,
It would at least appear to be concerning our
love matter,
I will submerge into a liquid,
That will cover me, my inner being, and
This will wash away the old, mar emotions,
Liquidate every impure residue of me and you,
It will present me cleansed,
Born again,
Revitalized,
Precious,
Un-scolded,
Delicate and lovely,
A sparkling gem,
Valued and treasured,
After the cleansing,
An anointed blessing,
Rare with qualities that only God
Gives,
Gave,
And will compose for all to behold,
Not an ending but a glorious, new beginning,
That starts first with God's never fading or changing
Words of,
"You are the one I behold and love with an everlasting
eternal love eternally,
And this, my love, will never fade or end."

SWORE

Here I am again,
And maybe you too,
Heart full of pain,
Night time dreary,
Daytime blurry,
Pitter, Patter tears fall down my, your
face like pouring down rain on window panes,
How could this happen?
I reassured my heart to never, ever fear
meeting in this state of derision again,
But here I am,
I was deceived by love,
Whisked away by a masterful, tantalizing, euphoric,
rapturous wind into loves clutches again,
Here I am,
And
Here I stand,

Here I go again,
Here you go again too,
Should I despise my feeling of loss?
Do I?
Should I cry until I understand?
Will I?
Should I pretend not to hurt within and walk
pass all while making proclamations such as,
"Ain't no thing",
Because,
Here I go again,
One thing is for sure,
I swear, this is the last for me and no more,
I gave my best and when this one ends,
This is surely enough and I say to you heart and on this
you can surely depend,
Never, ever again.

AT SOMEONE

I am looking at someone who use to love me,
Who I use too love too,
But love,
Our love,
That once was tender, sweet,
Our precious gift is gone,
Loves gone,
Loves gone,
It is not here anymore,
Love has gone far away,
I cannot remember just when the moment
or the day,
Someone and or ones are standing in our way,
Blocking,
Slamming,
Shutting love's door and forbidding the return
of it here ever again,
Love thugs I say,
Love thugs,
Brutal slayers,
Haters,
They despise the thought of it ever to
live here again,
Revive,

Unite two soul mates,
Two entwined best of lovers and friends,
Yes,
We had our struggles,
But never hate,
Filth,
Cruelty,
A sense of revenge,
These love thugs saw to it that it expired,
They would do it all over again, and again,
But no matter who,
Or what all they did,
No excuse for you, my lover, my friend,
No dearest,
Not at all,
I pronounce out loud again,
"You should have been my warrior until the end!"
Never allowing anything to happen to me,
Never I abandon,
So,
I just will be strong for the both of us until
the very end,
As I watch this love,
Our love, surely come to an end.

SILENT LOVE

Silent love has many facets,
It is when nothing is uttered,
It is simply all motions,
Not a mumbling word,
It can happen between two folks who
happen to sit next to each other,
An attraction takes place,
A look,
A stare,
It can transpire between two people sitting or standing
In approximation of each other,
Simply trying to keep warm from a cold wind storm,
Maybe down pouring rain,
The conversation stops or never starts,
Just looks, smiles and then suddenly passionate stirs,
As if out of nowhere,
Inner love materializes with charming, affectionate
desires,
Wanted hugging,
Touching,
Wanted kissing and the envision of making passionate
love,
It can simply be glances made from clear across the
room,
Ones from unattached souls yet to be connected,
Launched into what was heaven ordained,
Never, ever, even expected,
Meant to take away the sad feeling of loneliness and
gloom,

It can be caused by simple gifts given from your lover
or by someone whose heart that pleads affection
from you,
A powerful crush can and may materialize from a far,
However, this is more rooted in fascination and not
True, real love,
The healthy, mental outcome of these feelings will be
admiration, appreciation of that soul sent from above,
This may be one whom you could also have a genuine
attraction to, too,
Silent love is not rare and it can also give you the blues,
It can start with an adorable crush,
A strong, compelling force,
Many feelings that come like oceans of rushing
desires just to be with that person, or even a friend,
And somehow your paths cross and you do,
But then it also may be for someone who is attached,
Not open and free,
At first you may hate to admit it but everyone
around you
can see it happening, transpiring,
Just acknowledge it to your emotions and maybe a
comrade that is responsible, mature and cool,
It can be very uncontrollable at first,
Over powering,
And when you leave their presence,
There is a sigh of relief,
Especially if reality dictates no way,
Although the feeling is over powering, true,

Now you must get that rush under control,
Some call this impacting feeling a serious veneration,
Keep grounded, it will subside,
This will benefit your emotional growth,
Help develop your love sense,
And the crush may endure and be ever
so apprehending,
For when you see them you become enamored,
It is however a human experience that may happen
in your life more than once, more than a time or two,
It can be after stress and strife,
After I am not having anything to do with you,
After moments of not speaking,
Then love's heart beats over rules, over powers,
And because you are a true lover,
That love, lover is who you want, affectionately desire,
That, this love is what satisfies you,
Silent love is true love,
It is just as relevant and as powerful as the words,
"I Love You"
However,
Do not stay in or escape with silence as a way
of showing your love,
Too much of it forms an in balance in the expressions
and passion of what love is truly saying with words,
Projecting,
It can be irritating, frustrating, and disappointing
because
love still needs words, these words:
"I LOVE YOU"
But never say these words with false pretenses,

For you can rely on these words too console broken
hearts,
Help comfort them, help mend them again,
Facilitate emotional healing,
Do not say all of your "I love You " words to simply
strangers,
Or just anyone,
And,
Then never, ever repeat these words to who needs to
hear those, these vital, essential words most of all,
Your soul mate and love, intimate lover,
Silent love can be very delightful,
Enjoyable,
Sweet and wonderful,
Silent love, silent crushes,
Have the ability to bring together long
Awaited love that is right,
But may have been inconveniencing at the beginning
for whatever the reasoning,
This attraction is very real,
But,
This is not founded in criminal seizing of any being
for any mental in unbalanced feelings,
Unfounded justification for deranged violent, insane
actions toward any human being for aggrandizing,
Or self-gratification,
It is an expression of inner passion felt by both most
times,
It is indeed true love too love to be in,
Extremely powerful, very strong,
And,
It can and may endure for years and be very genuine.

CHRISTMAS GOODBYE

Silent days and silent nights,
This was the repeated, synopsis,
Of manifested, affirmed, prearranged
determined torturous plights,
Reiterated pronouncements of
these narrations,
No matter,
No matter,
The days and reshowing of days,
Or,
Night by night perilous plights,
What was the response to this delicate, fragile being?
Selected scenarios,
Selected fright,
The episodes unfolded,
She,
Tremendously scolded,
Tremendously scolded,
Silent days,
Silent nights,
After harrowing, violent outburst of
prearranged and rehearsed plots,
Homicidal scenes and plotted schemes,
Her husband indeed,
The husband indeed,
Not to mention all others with their
cunning schemes,
Unfaithful and hateful,
Hate filled,
Her, he jails,
Others accommodate with their violent rehearsed
Plots and schemes,
Their deranged pieces to their so called puzzle
themes,
Fulfilling his vicious missions,
Accommodated by witchcraft intruders in flight,
All others who envy what God meant for her delight,
He shakes his keys when entering daily,
Money the center of the reason to resent her,
Others with exploitation for the money matters,
Dauntless she still there,

Not always knowing just how or why,
Through pain, horror, and many times fear,
Just bold with grit and fortitude,
Just there,
No matter, no matter,
No matter the matter,
No matter,
Violent, schematic preplanned clatter,
Battered and shattered,
The laughter ensued greater,
The constant protest of haters,
Blocked and shocked by electric through
Evil supernatural realms,
Hexed and vexed,
Perplexed and stressed,
Some try to bless,
Nevertheless,
She is constantly disheveled,
The entire world in a state of derision,
In a complete mess,
Time to level,
And still until the clock strikes twelve,
Silent days and silent nights,
No longer does it appear to matter
the so called causes of constant terror,
The grim, impetuous, cannibalistic violators,
The perplexities, dilemmas,
All done for prearranged destinations and plights,
The goal to separate with the cruelest inventions,
Reckless intentions,
Why,
A name,
A life,
Chosen for not to be remembered,
Chosen not to be mentioned,
Blot it all out together,
Not ever to make it sounds the jealous,
No, no ascension,
Useless, worthless, not worth anything,
Not worth mentioning,
Not worth any money or time,

Blamed, shamed, treated insane, retarded,
All incidents inhumane,
They combine together to make her the cause,
With the intent to shut down her voice,
They bring to her constantly diabolical choices,
Presented as a remedy,
As a release from cruelties, atrocities,
And if in her rights she relentlessly remains,
Then shame, rape, spells and evil attacks day and night
in her
midst constantly persists, constantly remains,
dwells,
Stalkers, day time assaulters, rapist,
24 seven, not just at night,
They follow where ever she goes by media flight,
She, at times distraught, laments,
People walking in through the evil realms,
Dedicated to make her marriage,
Her life and existence pure hell,
Then,
Silent days and silent nights,
Outburst of violence to preset up violent plights,
Now the Christmas holiday seems just right,
To shatter God's rules,
To shatter God's word,
They say out boldly that she think that He
is coming back,
That He will return to a time when He boldly
loved and protected her,
How posteriors with bitter, contemptible envy they
Pronounce,
How absurd,
He is gone,
Moved on,
We did what was needed to bring about this day,
And so the ruling that was of a pretense daily
Outplayed,
Simulated parody,
No longer a charade,
Now seems ready to be presented,
Implemented,
After all it now appears the most relevant,
With underhanded evidence,
The most sensible outcome,

Best said all fuming traders,
Joyful backstabbers, plotters, assassinators,
Things were planned and worked out just
liked planned,
A means to an end,
Take away any money to spend,
And then she will need to bind to whomever
we send in,
And on welfare live and depend,
Frame, blamed with schemed, cruel sin,
We know just how to do this and
Win,
Intimidation is our best friend,
Applauds come from the ruthless,
horrid, virulent, slaughters with grins,
Complimenting their selves for their sins,
Over and over again,
Bragging to one another on social media and
with friends,
We will hand cuff her,
We will arrest her life,
Take her down,
Rape and assault her body, mind, and thoughts,
Leave her in violent filth, disease, drugs for need,
The pimps indeed will finally be pleased,
Rearrange and deprive, erase her God,
Erase her life,
Shout the bitter envious through strife,
They snarl at her blessings, talent, abilities,
God ordained given life,
And,
Because He, her husband she totally leans on
and depends, righteously loves, is mate to, is friend,
Now there will be, no doubt,
Justification for separation,
No reason to go on and him un-scorned,
No delay,
Why,
It is Christmas time,
May select to divulge on Christmas Day,
Must be before New Year's,
This is the way things will end,
A New Year,
Out with what was,

In with the new even if it is sin,
As long as it ends,
They forget that my God, Jesus, God
Of all hears and sees,
And so,
No longer will I lie down while I try to
do my best not to allow any to enter in here
ever again,
For the evil rapist use their media and their cars to
drive up
to rape here in,
And the witches month to do their
most evil deeds, cruel sins,
But really, all the time and it does not end,
Battling spiritual entities for days and nights,
Unending,
Through media as an entrance,
From where ever across the world, by beings,
Definitely from within the neighborhood,
And the community, just about by evil beings
everywhere,
Evil travelers now use electronic media especially to
intrude and invade atmospheres, travel to, come in,
The sad part is that this is not a new weapon,
Just very popular now with many to do violent,
Cowardly sins,
By the grace of God I will not innocently
accommodate
any schemes or plots,
Or buy by mistake any of their weapons,
These built and sent for the husband or me to select,
Another way to have them placed in our home,
Items needed to cause spiritual wreckage, havoc,
torture, death,
For it is not only evil appearing things used for spells,
But normal items appearing uncensurable,
Examples such as pictures and especially gloves
utilized for their hands,
And any kind of object that can be made dangerous,
Has power, can move, or cause harm,
They will try to drown you in a water scene if they can,

Push you off cliff edges and mountain sides from
pictures,
And under porches pin you in,
Electrocute you; assault your body parts,
All types of calculated harm and then some,
Drag you across muddy lawns,
Any and all kinds of ruination,
In here, concerning them, you see, all items
must be treated with scrutiny,
If or when we separate,
If the new mate proves not to be all that it seems,
If not,
She will know shortly in her visions and dreams,
Along with the attacks, and the arrangement of items
and things,
For her, to stay,
Would be insane after being attacked
daily by him and others in the supernatural realm or
and in any other violent scheme, scenarios, in any way,
He will no longer be her protector, no longer her
friend,
Yet, this is exactly how they desired this outcome to
to be,
The outcome to end,
Him involved in the violence,
Now before God,
Standing there trying to explain why He is
Now "Born Again" and unstained from
the previous, murderous plots of a former
eternal, ordained mate, love,
He does not feel that He will have to answer for
you see the word of God is now adjusted just like
when Moses was presented with ones such as these,
But this remedy is not sustainable before the eternal
Savior, Lord and King,
Goodbye is the sigh,
Be glad you did not die,
And so today this is what I say,
Be on your way,
Goodbye!

LOVE'S GONE

When It appears that love has ended,
And that there is no need for pretending,
Then if you lie about the matter to yourself and others,
This means that you are not your own best friend,
When it is gone,
You say so long,
And you forsake all your love songs,
All the sentimental whispers, lines and times,
To help ease your troubled mind,
And when the night gets long and cold,
You may find yourself missing that love,
And you may sing a song that you two loved before
the day dawns,
So how do you lose a love that was ever so strong,
And how and why does your white clouds
Now for you become gray?
And why do tears now stream from your face?
There will always different answers for each situation,
But know this my friend,

That those your clouds will turn white again,
Love renews itself over and over,
Love never ends,
Just like fresh morning dew on wet grass,
Sparking in the bright sunlight gleaming radiantly,
Love will do this for you too with uncontaminated,
new beginnings,
And many times, once your emotions have healed
And you are now ready to love again,
Because your heart is mended,
Love will not only be in the distance,
But very near, very close, real soon with rewards and
pleasure,
The happiness from a gracious soul mate only for you
meant,
Only for you Intended without false pretenses,
Remember have patience, heal, then you will win,
And then tears of sorrow and pain will turn
into joy once again.

TORN HEART

RIP,
RIP,
TEAR,
Now torn,
This is what you did to my precious heart,
Shred, Shred, Shred,
You cruelly shredded each and every
or any caring feeling,
Tears, Tears, Tears,
Down my cheeks are falling,
Because any love I would desire to feel for you is all gone,

How could you do this to me?
Why make me hurt and feel such void feelings for you?
I feel numbed.
The best thing is for me to let you be,
I will not let my heart ever become like yours,
And I will not let you hurt me again insensitively
with unspeakable hurt and pain,
This hurt comes from a heart that does
not love or care about me or anything we
had or cherished any longer.

My Yen

As I lay on my fluffy pillows and you too,
While we lay next to each other in bed,
Thoughts of you flow through my head,
Love we made and love we make,
Send beautiful, passionate heart desires,
Like delicate flowers falling with grace,
Like melodies expressing rhythms of fondness and
Compassion,
You are Yen,
I am appreciating the affectionate semblance,
Expressed care,
My soul is aware and conscience of these pleasures,
Such delicate rhythms in a harmonious atmosphere,
You color my world with your intense aura,

You are Yen,
Your male body, being created by the "Father" given
to me,
To be my soul mate, lover, companion,
To be eternal friend,
You are yen,
I accept your love theory,
I avow to its thesis,
My Godly mate, my love,
Not tragically,
But intelligently,
I profess this mind set,
Devoted feelings of endearment,
You are my yen.

I Love You

I love you because,
Your thoughts are beautiful,
Your actions are kind,
Your soul is righteous,
Our God is the same,
Our emotions, our hearts are entwined,
The way we love when we love results just the
way I love to love you,

Just the way two love mates who love each other
Should have the pleasure of experiencing and sharing,
A righteous, harmonious love,
Affectionate, God giving, caring moments,
Only yours and only mine,
Without intruders, a want to be, insane lunatics,
Violent rejects of any kind.

WEDDING DAY

Today is wedding day,
It came with a newness feeling,
It came with refreshing, moist fragrant dew,
The sky's sun radiates with sparkles like that of a
precious, rare, glistening diamond,
The sky is the most clarion blue,
Seemingly, just for our day,
Crystal clear without obscure views,
Anointed for me, and also my husband too,
After all the preparations,
Finally,
Our day has arrived,
My wedding day, Our wedding day,
My Johnny and I,
Now it is time to present this glorious dress,
To present it's purpose,
To give it it's grand display,
To look lovely, beautiful and quite elegant in it,
Surrounded by selected breath taking
flowers and candle arrangements,
The cake is sitting in its place looking classically
delicate, sumptuous, enticing and delectable,
The cake's appearance looks majestic, elegant,
alluring and dramatic on its crystal stand,
With water fountains and decorations of
the bride and groom, brides maids, flower girls,
ring barrier, groom's gents, maid of honor and best man,
And there are shawls that are anchored as they sway on
the pews where the guess will view all this very day,
The unique favors and tableware are in their places,
The band is ready and the hostesses are awaiting the
signal to usher folks to their appointed stations,
My face is beautified,
My hair is styled with loving, professional care,
Each curl is fastened tightly,
My Jews are rare,
I have my something blue and what I borrowed too,
My shoes now await my feet in them to appear,
I am surrounded by my portion of the wedding party
who attend to my every need,
They help out with such loving care,

I stop and say to all that it is time to say a prayer,
After that,
I said special words in private to all who I truly hold dear,
Now it is time to place my arm in whose arm that I
have chosen
to escort me down the aisle,
My dad awaits this moment but not as much as I,
My husband star gazes by the preacher and all the guest
as well with anticipation for the moment I am to appear,
The moment that I stroll down the adorned flowered isle,
And from that moment on,
Once I reach where He will be with gracious, peering eyes
and nervous speech, he then will be reaching out for my
hand as I for his also reach,
I will be united with my male companion and best
friend whose role
now becomes Godly husband, and I Godly wife,
It may have taken a while,
And yes,
There were some obstacles and delays along the way
and as time drew near,
But,
This is also nevertheless anticipated on most brides best
ever, spectacular, most ever glorious day,
Now we both walk to the preacher who will with patience
Be waiting till before him we stand,
As he tells us continue to join hand and hand,
Then He'll pronounce God's blessing,
As our vows before God we are confessing,
He will tell our lips to sink together where we stand,
Then he and others, our invited guest, will watch this
legal, beautiful, blessed union that is without
reprimand,
For a holy God commands and forms holy unions all
across the land,
And when the day is done,
And now it is just him and I as one,
We begin our journey in life together,
Together as one,
And yes,
We have only just begun.

My Love

My love, I just called to say how are you?
I hope that your day is going well,
As far as I know,

Our dinner plans are great,
Just try not to be late,
Love you!

AFTER

After ripping heart tissue that is
Bleeding all over the place
with rips of disgrace,

you say,
I love you.

22

What Is Your Love Color

What is the color of your love?
My love is a clarion color,
It flows like translucent pure rhythms constructing
a visible harmonious flow united with yours,
My love is flowing in harmony with the universe,
Always being refreshed by the creator,
My love is your pulse and fine, tuned rhythms of
your feelings blended congruently with tranquility
of emotions,
Yours and mine,
My love's color soars un-obscured,
Unhampered, Unimpeded,
By fog or midst or darkness that
exist,
It is clarion,
When the night star light in
heaven under it you, I with pulled
bodies share pure bliss,
My love is the color of naked,
Brassy,
Brown,
Bold,
Transparent,
It is indubitable,
Make no mistake,

Soothing for the intellect,
It is unequivocally, perceivably distinct,
It is nonnegotiable,
Luminous,
With moving shadows in still night,
Ours,
Yours and mine,
Pure,
Acquitting,
Forgiving,
Emancipating,
A deliberate, purposed delight,
My love is many colors,
After a glorious moment of surging,
erupting, explosive, tense and yet ever so
accommodating and pleasing, desirous love
sharing moments,
Moments that bring an explosion of colors,
Over my head and streams of cool blues
that are flowing through my senses as the wetness
and moister soothes my senses and moistens the
sheets and bed,
My love's color is simply clear and clarion,
And invested only
in you dear.

BREAKFAST

Eggs over easy,
Crisp, sizzling bacon and slightly singed ham,
Fluffy pancakes from hot skillet,
On plate 4 stacked high,
Dripping butter spreading from top to sides,
Warm maple syrup waiting for drizzle,

Juice, apple,
Tea, pleasing,
Letting out last yarn,
Yummy feeling talking to senses,
I eat through the morning conversation.

The Moment After

When all love's flurries are twirling
and the dewy mist of cologne
that existed and has faded, dissipated,
Moisten me with wet, soft lips,
Like the new morning mist,
The moment after,
My love, my soul mate,
My male spouse ordained and given to me by God,
Sooth gently, and pleasingly, and gently with
silky, smooth movements,
Enrapture me with your brazen, rapturous form,
With your soul, spirit, mind and emotions
expressing oneness, expressing pure love,
Caressing and giving all,
The moment after,
Wooing and gentle,
Fervent with care and comforting,
Then with powerful stirring movements,
Ignite passions as if unearthing yearnings,
As if being released from a heart
That waited ever so daringly starved
Of love so very, very, long,
As if of a soul that has just been granted
The privilege of swimming in oceans of
Pure, affectionate, gentle love, and unique blissfulness,
And yes,
It is so,
This moment,
My male sumptuous being given to me from God,
My soul mate, my love,
Underneath the fairest, velvet,
scenic covering sky,
Reaching and pleasing,
A bit of romantic teasing,
Preferred, seductiveness,
I am enamored,
Tender and heart yielding, I am,

The moment after,
Passionate, true moments are what I
want as due, beckon and desire from only you,
My male divine God ordained husband of mine,
The scene of some unskilled Romeo
is not the thrill,
Pretending to be there,
Masquerading care,
Never for me would be an acceptance or bring
sanctified
Blessed moments of love's euphoria,
Never ever pleasing, not here,
Forsake the dreadful, useless charades,
There are only, really, two heartbeats here that are
Being appraised, acknowledged, being celebrated,
Right here, right now,
In the presence of our Holy Father,
Just the same as the vows spoken to each other
On our God accepted anointed day,
Never waste a pure heart of love,
This is rare,
Love is not found or shared in everyone,
Broken hearts lie everywhere,
Each moment of true love shared,
Is a gift given,
Open it with delicate care,
Esteem,
Look sweetly upon and insulate
smitten memories there in,
Be fond of with benevolence,
The moment after you are granted my pure
Love,
Love me ever more,
Dote upon and adore,
Never, ever feel insecure,
The moment after,
The moment after.

Waiting Document

Together the rings,
The piano and organ plays,
The soloist sings,
The preacher has his say,
Yes,
A glorious, splendiferous day,
Before God almighty and the
angels the vows are said,
Before Yahweh,
The vows are made,
This is what we did,
Proclamation witnessed by
Allah and beings in heaven,
All promises voiced and read,
Waiting, all over,
Off into life they stroll,
The signed contract is now
tucked away,
Finances,
From him steadily flow,
Off to work he always goes,
Just the way the bible said that
it should be so,
Family business the anchor
thank God,
Shelters from devastations of
financial strains and
sorrowful woes,
Here she is,
Struggling not as planned,
Waiting on the right contingency,
Waiting on the fruition of well
thought out preparations and plans,
Giving financial support when able,
Although work hasn't yet proved
stable,
She is extremely gifted,
The best in just about all,
She just simply needs to
refocus some expectations and
explore diligently her creative prospects,

And then prosperity on her will befall,
She creates as God sees and is pleased,
Yet, He still provides the entire time
for her finances and it is so,
Patience as she goes,
Trusting, praying and believing
In her mate and the God she serves
and knows,
For him,
Waiting, this is not true,
Fortunately,
Economically,
These aren't his struggles,
Thank God because,
The future God does know,
He works and works with
little time for play,
A family becoming more
distant,
On passes the time, the years,
and days,
"We need God's help,
We need more time for us,
Together on our knees before
God's throne,
If this is ever to be,
"In prayer we must stay,
In prayer we must stay,"
This is what was asked,
This is what was pleaded,
Over and over again,
To prideful to listen,
To prideful to bend them,
This was not obeyed,
Waiting,
Waiting,
Time lost you cannot get back,
Not in the contract,
Miracles can be instant,
Come slow or not at all,
Depends on believer,

Depends on receiver,
Now she waits on you,
She waited for his transportation
for years to improve,
She helped with his schooling
And saw that he made it through,
When he had his break down,
She stood fiercely beside him still,
Not knowing the future and only
time would tell,
She reassured and as usual prayed
and supported,
She never abandoned him or complained,
When reality for him was distorted,
Just prayed him through,
Wives do not abandoned your mate
If he gets a bad break,
Pray him through and do not worry
Because if necessary the finances will
increase through you,
She stayed,
Always faithfully loving,
And managing the house,
He brought her many things,
The harmful ones He surely
should have left out,
In his mind,
Certain situations settle with
time,
Not good for reality,
Leaves out truth and important
beliefs,

For you see a view only from self
and improper advice,
Only ignites the enemies plan of
stress and strife,
The destruction of God's document
mandated for life,
Satan has one entitled too,
It is made for a couple,
Just right for the two,
Entitled "The Waiting Document,"
For what it entails is against God's
Solemn plan,
It is against God's will,
It puts undue pressure, tension and
expectations on the woman
or on the man,
Then a vicious, hateful, selfish, cruel,
cycle of thoughts and emotions pollute
God's system,
An inhumane sequence of events and
misfortunate circumstances underlying
in the conscience,
Manifest and destroy God's plans,
For the woman and the man,
Then, in reality they subsurface,
They damage and mishandle the
two's togetherness,
The woman and the man,
What was the plan or plans?
Can you actually blame one
or the other?
Who rejects God's wisdom?

Who with it ignores and actually
cares not to follow?
Why God blesses you as one unit,
God blesses you together,
The finances sent can come from
just one,
God clearly stated that the
woman is the helper,
That is why most often times
One person is the financial star
winner and the other is the creator
and supporter bar none,
Now springs forth on display,
"The Waiting Document,"
Just as the evil one planned,
Cunningly the advisors whisper
to the mate what to do,
All the disobedient one has to do
is listen and follow,
They know just how to instruct you,
What you will not see is the
consequences,
Heart aches, headaches, loss of

things you never anticipated,
At the end of the battle,
You still have not won,
You have lost it all,
You still have to face what
you tried to foolishly to
escape,
Then surely you will repent if you
are ever to reach and go through
those pearly gates,
The "Waiting Document" is the
One against the role and
Responsibilities that God has declared,
And so the disobedient mate then
declares that they are fed up and are
tired of waiting,
Because according to their expectations,
You are sadly mistaken,
The "Waiting Document,"
Signer beware,
It will cost you more than you ever
dreamed or ever dared.

ODE
MOON AND MOOD PHASES

There are eight phases
Of the moon like the many
moods of happiness and
sometimes gloom or the blues,
Especially if it involves the
Eternal vows made by two,
The first phase is called the
new moon,
The moon is not lit up by the
Sun at this time,
And it is not visible,
Like the way you feel when
In a relationship,
When your lover has become
distant and you wonder where
the lit light in his heart for you
has gone and has seemingly
disappeared,
The second phase is less than
half crescent,
Like when just a shimmer of
hope peaks out,
And lets you know that love
You cherish and have for him
no matter what is happening
is still there,
Even when there are thoughts

of giving up and walking out,
Then comes the half moon,
The sun is beginning to shine,
And the brightness of the sun's
light is getting brighter all the time,
Like the feelings that are beginning
To rejuvenate and stir,
And the true lover you once loved
And trusted appears to be apparent,
And not just somewhere still down inside
there,
The next phased is the half phase for sure,
And that is when the actions of love
Begin to change back to sincere and
Not disparity,
Not untrusty, and disgusts,
And, just simply give up,
But instead,
Patience,
Strength to further endure,
Sureness, and some feelings that
Makes you begin to somewhat
feel secure,
Then comes the full moon,
The moon is totally lit up by the sun,
This is when you finally have been
restored to the place in love,

Where you both dwelt,
And felt the warmth of love,
And where,
The radiance of happiness now lights
Up your inner heart and soul,
Your face illuminates with rays of love
Lights,
Your smile and cheeks give a beaming,
dewy glow,
The next phase gets smaller again,
Like in love,
It does mellow out,
And by the next phase yet even
Smaller,
The same as when you give space
To your lover,
You are not ambivalent at this
moment but you are okay,
Knowing that things are still alright,

And the last phase is when it is still
Just a bit of light,
The same as a relationship will
from time to time perhaps
Struggle with trying not to let
Loves light not fade away,
But,
To keep it blazing brazenly,
Even when there is an eclipse,
And one side of you is fuming,
Frenzied, vexed, saddened, glum,
While the other side is desperately
Still in love,
You have chosen,
To always give him your best,
Devotion, dedication and your heart,
Throughout each of your God
given lives,
As long as you both shall live and love.

Affectionate Real Love

What is real love?
Is it a demonstration of
Affection and care most of all?
Love is,
Emotional devotion,
Love is,
Enjoyment of yearned friendship,
Intimacy,
Holding dearly, passionately, with
fondness and fervor one's heart,
Love is gentle but with respectful, warm
touches,
For love never is brutish, unkind, or
a raving, violent, intrusive, aggressive bull,
Love never trespasses or pushes
its own agenda, or being,
It is splendorous and charitable,
You can give your all while enjoying the
journey,
It never settles for violence, or puffs
up when advances prove not there,
Love is,
Adulation,
Involvement,
Interesting,

Affectionate,
Romantic and precious,
Love is the giving of ones heart to
a lovely, pure heart that is waiting,
Love is,
Fascinating,
Captivating,
Delightful and prized,
It is cuddling with the soul you
are enamored with until the day
you die,
Love is the one you prefer,
The one you prize,
The one you are fond of,
The one you idolize,
The one you esteem,
The one you admire,
Are smitten by and adore,
The one you relish and hanker down with,
The one you hold, embrace,
caress, and protect,
It is the soul you are dear to and love,
The person you whole heartedly
give your allegiance to and like.

Absent Love

Absent love is love
you do not hear,
see, sense, entreat,
It has gone "A Wall",
Missing in action,
It is not cautious, and not
necessarily an unaware predicament,
entanglement, complication,
It is a MIA Lover,
Roaming the heart lands without appearance,
fondness or commitment,
Simply not there,
Heart without endearment,
It has no regard for care and
treasures hurt as a now tactical weapon,
It is obsessed with the flow
of streaming, aggrieved expressed tears from
the other mate,
And does not appreciate any past endeavors or
future whatever's,
It does not protect the heart or soul
against all invaders,
It is not necessarily interested
in another crusader,
It is absent and unpleasant,
It is demonstrated distress that was left
Unattended and therefore being expressed however
Long delayed,
However,
The MIA being,
Can be rescued,

They can be revived,
Without bitterness and harsh consequences,
Without letting them just die,
Appearing again and while staying lively,
And then flourish in the presence of
A heaven sent comforter,
Jesus, God the Holy Father,
But,
And if the soul is without emanation,
adulation, devotion and passion,
Then it is in dire need of restoration,
With help on its own, and with the help of loving,
gentle wisdom and God given patience,
This MIA,
Must acquire lost desires, feelings of devotion and care,
This soul must seek this on its own with the help of
prayer,
Once love goes silent, bleak, dies,
Often times it takes a while
Or what may appear to be forever to rejuvenate,
Restore,
And sometimes,
It just may never return,
It is gone.
It simply cannot be relived, revived,
It is no longer meant to be.
Let it go.
Recompose yourself,
Your life and emotional health,
It is time for you this to survive,

TRIBUTE
HUSBAND

As the husband
stepped over the
lower part of the grass,
first the right foot,
carefully,

then the left foot,
stepped down,
into the pit of
a rabbit hole.

LOVE THAT
Love That Man

Love that man like a steak and onions,
I said I love that man like mash and gravy,
Love to love him in the morning, noonday or
night,
I love to love my man with all of my might,

I love to call him my lovely one,
That's my man,
My husband John,
Why he is the joy of my life.
And I, Terri, I am his lovely wife.

ALL I WANT
ME

All I want is for you to love
me,
Love me with the heart of
God,
All I want is for you to not
attack but accept me too,
All I want is someone,
Someone who understands
how to love with the love of
God,
Not lust,
Not abusiveness,
Not deceitfulness,
But real genuine love,
Someone,
Without conditions,
For when conditions aren't
met,
Here comes the petitions,
Not someone delusional,
Demonic, controlling and confused,
Heartless, soulless, egregious,
Unprincipled, nefarious, low-down
And rotten,
A masquerading pompous fool,
All I want is someone to love me,
Love me with the love of God,

Someone who has no personal
agendas,
No unreal expectations,
No choking demands,
No really, sorry, no these are
my stipulations,
Someone who gives love,
Acceptance,
Affirmation,
Support unwavering,
Not in the background or foreground
Working evil towards me,
Being a foe and not a friend,
Being a,
An antagonist,
A defamer,
An invader,
Just a plain o' villain,
Then treat you,
As if you do not comprehend,
Someone who wouldn't want to
see me or anyone else without,
Scheme to auction and take what blessings
God granted me, was given, that I have,
That is without question mine,
Someone,
Who will sacrifice freely what they have,

And share with those in situations who may be pleading
for resources under God's leading,
Someone who relies on God to guide their
Actions, and doings daily,
And feels accountable to him for
their actions, activeness and decisions,
Someone who loves with a heart full
of compassion,
All I want is for them to care about,
Love me with the heart of God,
I want is for them to care about who I am,
To defend and protect my dreams and
accomplishments,
Without binding them or me to them
inside their prisons,

I want someone who cares,
Who for me prepares and not
abandons or leaves me in despair,
Someone who never stops making
sure that I succeed,
Someone who refuses to let me ever
not fulfill my dreams,
I want someone to love and protect me,
Someone whose motives are only blessings,
Not hurt, not pain,
No hidden agendas, cruelty,
deranged torture, or chains,
I want someone who loves me,
With unconditional love,
Loves me with the love of God!
Loves me with the heart of God!

BEST FRIEND POEM
JOHN

He is suits and singing where we go to hear God's word,
He is gulfing on a miniature course and while watching
him putting as he swings,
He is coffee in the morning as the donuts are swallowed
and consumed,
He is sweet candy anytime and especially late nights too,
He is a book well read that is a favorite to return to,
He is cologne that is now making a debut in our
Bedroom filling the air with his masculine choice of smell
enticement, alluring body fragrance,

He is the weight that He loves to lift up and down in his hands,
And with them he practices how to keep assailants away and me defend,
He is a motorcycle that speeds away fast and furious just to prove that he is hip,
also courageous and brave,
Not speeding from disaster or crime by him that was just created,
He is a car that drives me to restful places of assurance because of how I may tend to wonder if our love will always endure and never end,
He is news that is current and he always will be because he is my husband of 17 years now, 2017
My loving, God splendor of a man and best friend, my John, my J.C.

MINUTE
Longed

He longed for acceptance, love, respect,
He yearned for care,
Companionship,
A lover near,

He offered his heart, but with fear,
Hesitation,

Ambivalence,
Indifference,

He needs to be brave, fearless, strong,
Self confident,
Appreciative,
Accepting love.

Nonet
Love Time

Love's yearning is a lament, desire,
Fondness, devotion, yielding choice, crush,
A flame undaunted, lover freed,
Following after one's heart,
Cherishing real moments,
No infringement here,
No pretense, lies,
Just passion,
Regard,
LOVE!

SONNET
Come Love

Come my love and explore my affectionate joy,
Come lay in splendor only met for you, my love,
I lay here longing for your sweetness to enjoy,
Oh how the moments will bring obeisance, thoughts of
Pure bliss, and I do miss, the touch of your warm flesh,
Entwined from the very first moments of desire,
From the moment I wanted no other, my best,
Your splendor I never tire, just admirer,
Now you have beckoned with such tenderness, fervor,
Wanting nothing but the omnipotent one's choice,
We love cherishingly, righteously, adoringly,
Your voice is wooing with soft, calming, words for heart,
Aspirations, tenderness, raptured, no depart.

LANNET
Sunset Love

Dwindling, receding blue fading, rapt,
Scene fades, present lower, duskiness lights,
Sensibility soothes the passions yearned,
Midnight may find mortals entwined, cleaved,
Sand, terrain, beautified by stars, moon, souls,
Shadows breathing in allure, temptation,
Panting heart beats of seductiveness, lure,
Gleaming tides sweep away will, flaming love,

Streams of pleasure, affections, flames prevail,

Wonderment at last, appeasing senses.

Where Are The Love Moments

Where are the love moments,
Nights spent with cheese and
Sparkling drink,
Love kisses,
Love touches,
Splendid times we shared my
Nubian prince,
Where are the times we spent,
Going places, sharing graces as
around the cozy booths like
where we first ate,
Where we always went,
Where are the sweet, smooth cheeks
that often met beneath the sheets,
That adoring masculine frame that
embraced this fair womanly body,
Where are the heart pounding times
Of just sitting with your hand entwined
In mine,
As we talked about the future,

And looked forward to being together
In time,
All the time,
Viewing the future with
Optimism, expectation, trust,
Fiercely stating that nothing will
Ever break us up,
Do our hearts need a jump start
Again,
How about a love solution that
Removes all pain,
All the past mistakes,
Making a focused, true effort to
be happy again,
Doing nothing to hurt or ever injure and
endanger neither one ever lover,
Going before God and giving Him all,
Because in Him we will find all that
was ever lost.

I Am
Your Lover

I am your lover,
Your dearest flame,
I am your sweetheart,
Your true friend,
I wonder if you are my
beloved,
My admirer, beau,
I fall into your arms
like a lamb,
Trusting devotedly your
plans while doting about
you to friends,
My Nubian, masculine man,
My prince charming,
My husband,
I hear sweet sounds that
make my heart flutter as
you talk tender with that andric
voice,
I see two smooth souls floating
across waves of symphonic,
flowing motions of dewy, love
passions during romantic intimacies,
I want only you ever more,
No pretending here,
I am your heartthrob,
I am your idol,
My love will shield you from
those who try to do you in,
I pretend that we are two lovers
In a wonderful, elegant mansion with
servants at our beck and call,
with chefs that fix whatever we
want and desire,
But yet how we are right now
Is awesome,
I have you and you have me,

And,
between us both dwells God
with His protection and His
unending love,
I feel cool streams of misty
fragrant cologne when
In my ear you are whispering
sweet nothings to me,
Spraying an enticing mist on
the very words you speak,
And then I touch and turn your face
as I pull it closer to my face and lips,
I worry for nothing in moments like
this,
I cry when I think that I
Am not by your side to
know that you are okay
sometimes and cannot
wait until I see that things
are alright,
Simply fine,
I understand that you do
love me and are giving and
provide for me all that you can,
I say prayers for you, us, constantly,
So that we stay united as God planned,
I dream of all that we have not seen yet,
I try to remember that God will and God can,
I hope that you continue to get sweeter than pure
honey
and nectar so that my cravings for you never end,
I am your honey,
Your true love
Your soulmate,
We are one,
A Godly union.

Haiku
Anniversary
Anniversary
Champaign, Roses, Money, Card,
A day to enjoy!

When I Think OF

When I think of love,
I think of you, John,
I think about all the fun we shared and share together,
Just "Me and You,"
When I think of goals, dreams, and all sorts of
important things,
I am definitely thinking of you too,
When I think of an achiever, someone impressive,
intelligent, and yet
they still are someone who loves to smile and adore me,
I am thinking graciously of you,
When I am thinking of a wonderful future and
although there will be some
Challenging moments and times,
Yes, again I am gazing at a future with you,
But what is a struggle without you by my side,
So yes,
I am definitely thinking about you with all my heart
and mind,
When I think of our first moments together,
Our first class at college,
Our first words spoken,
Our first gaze,
My first pitter, patter in my heart for you,
Our first ride in your ride,
Our first dinner,

Our first date,
When we first held our hands together while so
deeply, affectionate, and in love,
The first time you were standing at the alter waiting for
a bride for
your very first and only time and I,
So deeply in blissful love walking down the church
aisle to my first
and only, God given husband for the very first time, I,
A God daughter bride,
I yearn with sweet desires of those moments,
That can only be repeated with you,
Our first wedding for us both,
And you know, I will always love you, love you now
and forever only besides God,
And outside of myself the most,
I remissness us saying our vows before the preacher for
the very first time,
And all of the rest of the ceremony as I saw it unwind,
I thank God for you my beloved husband,
John David Cunningham,
A leader, provider, loving, awesome,
A sweet chocolate that belongs to no one else but me,
How fortunate I am that you are mine,
Love you now and always,
My adorable Valentine.

STEAM ROLLER LOVE

Like a steam Roller,
Your love swiftly,
And with powerful force,
Rolled over my emotions,
Crushed my strength,
Shattered my defenses,
And obliterated my will,
It left me vulnerable,
Somehow, I found my strength to get up again,
Although disoriented,
I found my fight, my will,

My ability to find solace and inner peace brought back
The joy and smile I once had,
This changed my plight,
And love's renewing streams sent waves of soothing,
crystal clear,
Gleaming, illuminous healing waves that soothed, and
cooled,
My tenuous, uneasy spirits,
It made me whole,
I was comforted,
My inner emotions are no longer out of control.

BLUE BONNET

He wants me to wear the bonnet right now,
They all in need of greed tell him right now,
He is getting the wizard gang from
Social media, town,
The president and all the gents that be,
The politicians, musicians, those in the community,
They act as if God is sightless,
They act as if God don't hear, don't care,
They attack the mind, the brain, entire being,

They want me dead to steal works, achieving's,
My health, life, mind, strength, safety, God's keeping,
Priceless talent, wit, charm, strength, God gave that,
Intelligence, purity, God gives that,
Humbleness, vision that you can't take back,
I put my trust, hope, faith in Christ whose there,
I trust the Lord Jesus, cause things aren't right,
Situations are inhumane, illegal, violent, unfair.

ODE HORATIAN

A Love Fool
You think I be your nincompoop, love fool,
You think your gimmick I am not aware,
You think dare I demarcate, ascertain you,
And that I surmise it is true love that we share,

For whatever its' equivalence, worth, you served,
Truth will not obscure, hide, adumbrate it within,
The smiles, called for assail, pummel, you reserved,
Did give passage to disdain, disparagement friend.

You Are The Best Love

Flowers and Showers,
Candlelight and Movie night
Motorcycle riding and Track walking
You are the best Love,
Rock climbing and Sky Diving
Amusement Parks and Pick nicks
Horseback Riding and Slay board sliding
Roller Skating and Love Making
There is always something to do with you,
Like wine and cheese and a romantic eve,

Or just simply snuggling beneath the sheets,
You simply are interesting and know how to
Please,
And with me you even dare to go shopping,
Exercising and bike riding,
And when the day is done and we say our
Prayers together to glorify God,
That is always what I love most of all,
You are the best love,
As good as they come.

COUPLETS

The Glow
In my heart a love does glow, radiate,
When you appear it illuminates bright.

The Bubbles

These bubbles await your plunge, your male bud,
I am already splashing with joy, suds.

Intense Love

The wonderment of euphoric intense love,
How enraptured, ambrosial, to be.

Lover

Forever delectable, entrancing,
Your love style speaks, paradisaically.

Tetracty

YOU ARE LOVE

ove,
You are,
My yearning,
My very breath,
The existence of what I need to breath.
There is no other beloved delight,
That sets me free,
You are joy,

Pure bliss,
Hope,
You,
Are soft,
Gentle and kind,
My solicitude,
Obeisance, respect, love, regard I give.

Every Day Poems

THE MOAN OF A MOM

Sometimes moms moan,
They lament,
They groan,
They cry,
They sigh,
They whimper,
They bewail,
They simply may have to at different times
burst out into tears,
Most times when this happens,
No one is around but the Lord,
No one but Jesus,
Or,
Often times their best friend, or friends,
And Sometimes,
People from afar and folks who come
And gather from very close, very near,
Often times this moan is an outward
display of a piercing, heaven penetrating groans
right then and there because the pain of the
situation is too hard,
To unreal,
To catastrophic,
Much too painful,
Much too grievous to bear,
When a mom's true, real, sorrowful
complaint fills the room that she is in,
Heaven stops,
Jesus takes notice,

The angels watch intently,
God, Our Father, sits up on His Throne in His
Majestic Chair,
Heaven, does know the situation before on earth it
unfolds,
You may think they do not see it, are unaware,
Father God, Jesus, the angels and the angelic family,
You may even think that it goes unnoticed,
They see it, they know the matter, they are right there,
When in the midst of the perplexity,
Sometimes it is such a lost feeling of how can such a
concern of mine be of importance,
After all, do not the uncountable situations
of sorrowfulness reach the "Throne of God"
all at the same time?
So,
How does each one, somehow, individually
become especially noticed,
Be given heedfulness,
Intentness,
Diligence,
Consideration,
Reflection,
Exclusive application of care,
Monumental devotion from the "Heart" of
a "Majestic God",
Most importantly, particularly mine,
But,
Nevertheless,

Jesus is always interceding on our behalf,
He is great at this,
He does this best,
So,
Way before the first moan,
Sob,
Grievance,
Is petitioned and the onset streams of tears
roll down the face,
or,
Sunken cheeks,
And maybe even tossed about hair,
Jesus took the complaint to "The Father",
And although it happened,
Because of a world of sin we dwell in,
You are not without God's comfort,
God's mercy and kindness,
God's care,
His attention to the matter,

His solution if you accept it,
And love no matter what,
His closeness to you and the situation,
And special consideration because the aching,
Distressing,

Bemoaning,
Mourning,
Disquieted,
In consolable, sorrowful, weeping heart of a Mom,
Mum,
Mater,
Momma,
Mommy
Mother,
Is one that God gives His undivided attention too,
He grants His, responsive, dutiful, considerate,
attentive, loving, kind ear.

JUST NEED TO RUN

I just want to run,
As fast as a jet,
In fact,
With the speed of a jet,
Just like that,
I want to fly through the midst of it all like
An airplane leaving behind all that ales me,
Woes and pines,
All who are vindictive,
All the unkind,
All the mean,
Abhorrent,
Infamous,
Heinous,
Abrasive,
Venomous human being kind,
King David, He had to run from Saul,
He ran through valleys,
Over mountains and pathways,
And ran until he was delivered from all problems,
From all ills,

I want to run like David until all sickness is gone,
Until those who want to change my name and status
are the ones who are long gone,
Until the Me, God created being is celebrated instead,
I just need to keep on running until there is no more:
Unrest,
Cruelty,
Threats,
Jealousy,
Fear,
Dread,
The envious are not satisfied until I am dead,
Run until all realize the suffering of the cross,
And that they need King Jesus,
And to proclaim the righteous cause,
And to accept Salvation and Jesus as Lord,
I just need to get out of here,
And run until they too decide to follow to
pick up the cross.
To serve him boldly, all without fear,
Living born again free and not lost.

Another Soul

Another soul flew away today,
The cruelty of bullying is
tragically still the enemy and device
of choice used to accomplish the precious
waste of God given life daily,
And so now the angels part the heavens
and welcome another vexed, precious soul on the way,
I still do not care rages the possessed humans
in need of God's guidance and caring ways,
Have you no love in your heart at all?
What about a bit of empathy and sympathy please?
How about some humbleness?
How about some prayer?
How can such little ones continue to behave
in such awful ways?
Who has failed? Who is the blame? Is it me, you, us?
Surely it is not God and so we all must take a stand
against
this or take the blame,
Generate love to all daily and not misery and shame,
Compliment and not ridicule which creates toss a
ways,
Give guidance, structure, encouragement, and love,
Teach right from wrong and demonstrate this openly,
And,
not just speak about it as if it is uncommon, uncool
attributes
not really needed at all,
Don't compromise and choose just a few who
this will be given gladly, compassionately,
and definitely too,
How will the young ones change if the adults

are acting out the same mannerisms and with love
only for
a chosen few,
The changes begin in the leaders, guiders, shepherds,
And that means our local and national pacesetters
and not just me and you,
Start becoming involved again in every aspect
of life that comes across your path,
That you can positively impact,
Make good efforts, affects, and changes, Give love,
Care and watch for the travelers,
Jesus said that this is necessary, mandatory, best,
We are not called to be perfect,
But we are called to care, respect, love and forgive,
To help out one another in this world where we all live,
To teach Godly principles and we must apply them
first and foremost
To our own lives,
To our own opinions,
To ourselves,
To our self and those we claim and give life to that are
born,
Love travels along way and you too will need it on
many a day,
Especially the times of bitter mockery, scorn, and
downward turns,
Caring is the new fashion so try it on and wear it well,
Throw away your bully outfit,
It is an awful outfit, garment with a terrible
constructed, mill dew fabric in dire need of riddance,
A drastic toss away.

Something Is Broken

Slit, Slit,
You may not get this,
Slit, Slit,
That is just a mournful, gripping, display,
Affliction, crucifying addiction,
Scars it always bears on the skin,
 Blood oozing, nullifying weariness,
State of flesh rare with aching
wounds baring the pains I incubate,
Inside, hollow, blurry tomorrow,
Slit, slit, burn, burn,
Why?
Something is broken,
No one to hear,
No one to understand,
No one to care,
Sometimes burns,
Depending upon whose hurting,
Out of their despair,
Somehow this is what I'll do to declare,
Something is broken,

Miss it, dismiss it, condemned,
Injury, laceration, complications,
Wounded inside, wounded outside,
Annoyance to acknowledge,
Pestering, embarrassing at best,
So how do you handle this so called
Aggravation,
Bothersome, excruciating, exasperating,
Inflaming, injurious, vexing ordeal,
How do you approach?
How do you begin to embrace, face this harrowing,
complex, yet reachable heart and soul sickness?
One loving word at a time,
One loving I love you at a time,
One I'll listen and let you talk at a time,
One Jesus is the answer who is always ready to listen,
care, be there when no one else is at a time.
One I am here and do care to listen at a time,
How do you reach a soul, heart, that is crying out from
a living purgatory?
One loving, saving answer at a time.

Struggles

When it seems like struggles,
When it seems like your struggles,
When it seems like "The Struggle",
Has entrapped, entangled, repressed,
Restrained you in on all sides,
Just break through those barricades,
interferences, mocking's,
and despair,
Just be brave and break through,
When it seems like tomorrow does not
awaken you with bright, bold sun rays,
That warms your heart and soul with inspiration
for the day,
And, then send you graciously on your way,
Just trust and believe,
Affirmation is only delayed,
Just let your faith and bright smile radiate
the path you are destined to take,
In this world we are born to folks called family,
There are other folks who dwell here too called,
Friends,
Neighbors,
Associates,
And those passing by whom you greet,
All these folks will either help or try to hinder you
and all the dreams that you have chosen to pursue,
It then becomes easy to fret,
Lose faith, and angrily react,
But listen to your inner voice,
Echoing from your soul,
Hold tightly to the vision comprehended and given,
And never, ever let them go until you achieve,
accomplish your goals,
Soaring high and flying on your own,
Put your shoes on,
Try them on,
Wear them proudly,
There used to be a time when they were new
that you had to trace your feet before they
were worn,
Struggles,

Struggles,
You had to trace around your feet before they were
worn,
Remember "The Struggle",
Remember "The Struggle",
Don't worry about the spells,
Don't worry about the sorcerer,
Don't worry about the scorners,
They are destined for hell,
They are destined for hell,
Struggles,
Struggles,
Will never, ever go,
They may be different from person to person,
Or stay the same despite the complications and
sorrows,
Nevertheless achieve,
This is your destiny,
This is your destiny,
Religion,
Education,
Rights,
Upward mobility,
Freedom and freedom rights,
Freedom to live safely without persecution,
and violence, prejudice, bias, illegal decisions or
disgrace,
Freedom from violent attacks with in your culture or
others especially your kind and race,
Freedom to rest,
Freedom to sleep and dream,
Freedom to serve God the almighty,
Freedom to dwell with your husband mate given to you
from his throne,
And not a worldly designated, illegal God forsaken,
unapproved,
Scripture objectionable, interjected being,
God's Holy Spirit of Judgment will reign indeed,
Sometimes you may not realize that you are in a
struggle,
"The Struggle" or your "Struggle",

It may just seem like you keep having a difficult time,
But when hard times are prolonged too long,
Then it is a "Struggle or "The Struggle" indeed,
Whether or not you perceive it or believe it,
Acknowledge it,
Face or embrace it courageously,
It is still a struggle or "The Struggle",
It is still your struggle or this "Struggle",
Whenever not just regular folks you encounter and see,
If the matter involves unjustified powers,
Spiritual warfare and hells demons that be,
When attacked physically, financially, and in your
dreams,
When they all band together and assassinate
everything you try
or have accomplished and achieved,
This means that the force coming against you is
embedded in
human cruelty, and spiritually,
When they rape you boldly,
Call you a fraud and illegally tape and jail you just
because
You serve God,
Attack you violent and unspeakably,
Without conscience at all,
Just know that this happened too to just more than
just one
Individual,
And such others as:
Martin,
Harriet,
Frederick,
Malcolm,
Ralph,
Alvin,
Sojourner,
Crispus,
Arthur,
Just to name a few,
The righteous are:
Jesus,
John,
King David,
Paul,

Silas,
Peter,
The children of Israel, The Hebrew Servants, The Jews,
Matthew, Mark, Samuel, Luke and more than
likely you,
For the struggle is not only for a particular culture or
being,
It includes everyone from where the struggle is or has
taken place,
Male or female,
Any culture, any place or time in history that has been,
Transpired,
It may include your own culture and people,
This was how slavery became prominent and
dominant,
No matter the circumstances,
No matter the pain,
Don't feel ashamed,
Remember,
Before you consider all discouragement, bleakness,
Despondency, predicaments, and setbacks,
Take one more look at your leaders,
Take one more look at your ancestors,
Take one more look at your accomplishments
and endeavors,
Then righteously thrust forward,
And shake off as much bitterness from the struggle
As you go,
Bitterness is rooted in frustration and anger,
Disappointments and many woes,
However,
These obstacles have proven never to stop destiny
although it destiny it may interfere with, make
frustratingly slow,
Hindrances are made to turn into victories,
They beam splendidly once the obstacles are trampled
upon and gone,
Struggles,
Struggles,
Hindrances,
Obstacles,
Are victories like smiles and frowns,
Simply turn them upside down.

Stairway To Jesus

Although I walked this realm many a life given step,
Although I caressed your face and dried your
tears on many a day that you wept,
I will always do the same, no matter where I am,
Even though I am in a heaven destined plain,
Not the same, but yet I do and always will remain,
Above the clouds,
I know me right now you may not be able too
see, envision, or even perceive my presence,
But,
Just know that although you weep, I hear and I do
understand your grief,
And one day, yes, you will be here with me living
in heaven,
And with Jesus and then we both will be ever so happy,
Again,
So,
When you see a floating cloud just know that,
I am resting in Jesus.
I am resting in Jesus.
I know that you are hurting and grieving,
I know tears are streaming,
I know that your heart aches and breaks,
And, you may also be thinking was it something that
you could have done,
NO!
We all have a destiny at an appointed time,
Each and every one,
This, anticipate,
No matter the circumstances, no matter,
Our days are accounted for under the sun,
Then,
The stairway to Jesus we must then climb,
That bright lit journey that is heavenly devised,
Away from all life's pressures, expectations,
dire situations, sorrows, struggles,
But not all strain,
There was also success, love, joy, and divine happiness,
Most of all,

Mainly,
My love for you all too, that is and will never, ever
change,
Especially for you, dearest,
Most of all in your heart of love I will always too
remain,
I gave my all and many a soul it blessed,
My Jesus knew my needs and granted what was best,
Divine rest,
Hear me as I sing,
Yes Jesus loves me,
Yes Jesus loves me,
And this I leave and all my worldly treasures for
a realm far better,
So when you think of a bright sunny day,
My love will comfort and light your way,
When the breezes blow softly in Spring,
When the songs of the birds you hear singing,
And when on fresh falling snow the sparkles of sun
rays glisten,
And when in your mind me you are missing,
Sing a song with me and my love will sparkle like
gleaming sun rays,
 comfort like soft, warm Spring breezes,
and bring melodies of joy and love from the birds
you'll hear singing
In the daylight,
A blanket of velvet sky that covers the earth with
stars is where I'll gleam,
To watch over you as you dream,
I'll be next to Jesus night and day,
In His eternal presence,
And in your love, I will, as I mentioned always stay,
But until you are able to see my smile,
hear my voice again and I yours,
Just know that I walked the stairway to heaven,
And that Jesus greeted me,
And all of heaven's host proclaimed,
"Welcome Home" dearest Whitney.

Reminder

Yet another reminder,
Oh No!
Fallen!
Moments surreal, time stood still!
Pondering! Stunned! Locomotion!
Mind in vague, trance time,
Cartilage now begins to lye,
Lifeless osseous matter transpired,
Obsolescence,
Expired,
Cessation,
Souls flying all at once to the sky,
Violence, annihilation is here,
Tragedy not scarce,
Tragedy not rare,
Death too now here,
Still dismayed today,
Gone away,
Suddenly,
Alarm,
Tumultuous travesty,
Far gone,
No win,
No win again,
Reminder of kinder,
Reminder of care,
Your still here,
Not gone, not gone,
By the grace of God,
Meditation and prayer,
Souls flew away while bodies lied
motionless as they fell,
Fly away beyond the clouds,
Gone away, gone away now,
Our town of tears applicable here,
Smiles turned upside down,
Inconsolable hours,

Flowers to lie,
Teddy Bears and candles on display,
Cards with expressions and posters
beside each other lay,
Hugs for pain,
Now the blame,
No words alleviate grief,
Now time stands still before it flies
with cries,
Empathy,
Sympathy,
Far better to care,
Acceptance,
Perhaps passion,
Too late,
Consequences of hate,
Perpetuated state of hate,
Avoidable fate,
Now a soul is through the never to return gates,
Never to return gates await,
Frigid, bleak state,
At best the rest,
Left with recoiling memories of pleasant,
special occasions all now cherishing,
Bitter sweet,
Bitter sweet feelings now you keep as you weep,
Reminder to love,
Reminder to care,
Empathy,
Sympathy,
Acceptance,
Respect,
Your still here, not gone,
Not gone,
Reminder,
Reminder,
Reminder to read God's word, obey it, love and care.

Tornado

Twirling,
Swirling,
Whirling,
Round and round,
Picking up and throwing houses,
cars, buildings, structures and objects
violently to the ground,
The trees split,
The wind blows with fierce force and forms
a rapid rotating funnel twist,
Objects are spinning around, above and within
the funnel's vortex inner midst,
Hail and rain usually accompanies this wind storm,
However, it does appear with just magnanimous
clouds and winds alone,
It shatters glass and any and everything fragile in
its path,
Take shelter or you will be caught up in the winds
fierce blast,
Folks take shelter and hover inquisitively in areas
that are deemed safe,
Hoping that the winds by pass their space,
Meteorologist call them twisters or cyclones,
It is a ripping, roaring, rotating dangerous column
of air,
The term super cellular refers to when it develops over
bodies of water and only there,
It connects to the surface of the earth and a
cumulonimbus cloud,
The narrow end of the funnel touches the earth
and grounds,
Lightening will appear in spurts,
And it is accompanied by debris and dust or dirt,
Then when all the wind is gone,
It is time to repair all the damage that is done.
Hopefully, none of your kin and friends were tossed
by the storm,
And yes, by your side and in your arms they all
are left as well you unharmed.

PROSE

Revealing The Enemy

Some people read your poems for inspiration. That is what I do also when I choose to read anything that any one writes. However, everyone does not read what you write for that reason. They read your writings to bring about destruction to you by wicked spiritual means. They use your own words and any images to try and attack you. They love and depend on patterns of three in any form. They blow out your light bulbs. This is usually someone who is definitely attacking you and they are using an image. It is that person. They use tools to change your insides like a doctor. This very well may be a doctor or nurse, or dentist attacking you. They will also arrange your clothing, food, anything in your house including your shoes. Try to bury you in mud, trap you inside doors. They invade you through visions while you sleep. Nothing is off limits including rape. People in your house may also be helping out. Your neighbors may also have a key to your place to arrange your house while you are gone. Exposing their methods is what you need to do constantly. Spiritual warfare is very real. Sometimes the person is unaware of the attacks taking place. A lot of times they will simply use the image of that person that is in the form of a picture or pictures. Just remember to expose their methods. What must you do? Be very careful what you write and images you choose to use. No, you are not delusional or losing it. The goal is to bring a gutter ending to your existence. Utter disgrace and shame. Sorceries are here indeed. No you are not paranoid.

We are human, but we don't wage war with human plans and methods. We use God's mighty weapons, not mere worldly weapons, to knock down the Devil's strongholds... break down every proud argument that keeps people from knowing God... conquer their rebellious ideas, and we teach them to obey Christ. (2 Corinthians 10:3-5 NLT)

[19] The acts of the flesh are obvious: sexual immorality, impurity and debauchery; [20] idolatry and witchcraft; hatred, discord, jealousy, fits of rage, selfish ambition, dissensions, factions [21] and envy; drunkenness, orgies, and the like. I warn you, as I did before, that those who live like this will not inherit the kingdom of God. Galatians 5 New International Version

Nahum 3:4

all because of the wanton lust of a prostitute, alluring, the mistress of sorceries, who enslaved nations by her prostitution and peoples by her witchcraft.

PROSE

Enemies Exposed Through Spiritual Attacks

Noises in your house or spiritual wicked enemies running around in the form of demons are real. Folk coming in your home by evil realms is a very real factor too. You made me mad. I will avenge my way in a spiritual form. As soon as you shut your eyes, that is when they attack mainly. They do also attack when you are awake as well. But mainly when you are asleep. Anything goes. You must be conscience of that. What are some of these attacks or what might they do? I'll tell you. They are violent physical assaults. They are violent dream attacks. Do they try to kill you? You bet ya. This could be most anything: battery to batteries, black spelled words and black objects, things left plugged in, and images designed by their selves, they love to be snakes, they fly by bird pics, they are extremely upset if you they can't control you or run you out. God help you if they want to marry you. They set up illusion divorces and illegal unions over and over again. Like beetle juice. They will attack your health, features and anything else. This includes pulling out your teeth. Making you gums bleed and hitting you with things. You do not have to make an enemy. They use containers filled with stuff to put inside of you like hair pomade or anything else. They use the lines under your neck to put things in your body like water in water bottles. They will turn you into an animal. They will make you make animal sounds. Move like animals. They will make you act like another person. How? By the images left in open view. Sounds crazy right. Well this is how it looks on the surface. This is what they are depending on to have you locked up and put away for life. This is why I am writing this in this prose format for all those who have experienced this or who later on will. They will arrange socks in a draw like the filling in your molar teeth. Then they will come along when you are sleep and try to pull your tooth out. They will also arrange socks in white color in the shape of teeth as well. Remember, it can be quite frustrating and this is why a lot of people do snap. Now if you do not have good dental hygiene from the start, you are a perfect target. They just could want what you have. In another instance, your spouse could want a divorce and chose tormenting as his means of handling you. They will bring home objects that they can manipulate and when you approach them, they show a sincere I have no idea what you are talking about face. This includes folk's children, they include them as well. Instead of raising them to serve Jesus, they are raised to attack you. Will they rape you? You bet ya! They use objects in your house. This includes all of the above. They stand in your yard, sit in cars, and work inside and out through images and what they have placed in your house. Anything with images and anything that is a power source. They also will place you in Human Trafficking. People from the net will come in your house as well through this realm by phone, tablet, etc. They use your web sites for their Human Trafficking. So, be careful of your enemies. They use all forms of the media. Nothing like having connections everywhere. Except for Jesus, you may very well be a lost cause. They are on every level. From the political level that will get involved and visit there too, folks incarcerated, your neighbors, Companies and ordinary folks who walk down your street. Sadly, your family. I use to wonder how the scripture would be fulfilled when it said that because iniquity shall abound, the love of many shall wax cold. Your enemies will even be of your own household. What better way to achieve this then through evil realms. The enemy is very cunning. They smile in your face and violently attack you to shame and disgrace.

- Finally, my brethren, be strong in the Lord and in the power of His might. Put on the whole armor of God, that you may be able to stand against the wiles of the devil. For we do not wrestle against flesh and blood, but against principalities, against powers, against the rulers of the darkness of this age, against spiritual hosts of wickedness in the heavenly places. Therefore take up the whole armor of God, that you may be able to withstand in the evil day, and having done all, to stand. Stand therefore,
  - having girded your waist with truth,
  - having put on the breastplate of righteousness, and
  - having shod your feet with the preparation of the gospel of peace;
  - above all, taking the shield of faith with which you will be able to quench all the fiery darts of the wicked one.
  - And take the helmet of salvation, and the sword of the Spirit, which is the word of God;

praying always with all prayer and supplication in the Spirit, being watchful to this end with all perseverance and supplication for all the saints — and for me... (Ephesians 6:10-20 NKJV)
KJ21
And 'a man's foes shall be they of his own household.'

VISION

You can only dream what you envision,
You can only envision what you really desire to be,
You will only achieve what you,
Honestly,
Realistically,

Passionately,
Assertively,
Intelligently,
And sometimes desperately pursue,
Be it unto me.

My Mom's Sayings

Momma's say things like,
"You can be anything you want to be if
You set your mind to it,
"I am going to make you see stars,
What if everyone jumped off a cliff,
Would you do it too?
"You will know the next time,
"Eat those carrots they are good for your eyes.
They make your eyes pretty,
"If you can't say something nice,
Don't say nothing at all,
"I will knock you into the middle of
next week,
"I hope someday you have children just like
you,
"The little bird told me what you did it,
"Put on clean under ware,
You will never know if you will be in an accident,
"I'm just talking to hear myself talking,
"I'm gonna give you till the count of 3, 1, 2....
"You have to excuse your father,
"Do not cross your eyes,
They will freeze that way,

"Who said you could do that?
Did you get my permission?"
"You do not know up from down?
"Close my door! I am not heating up the neighborhood
and you can't pay the bill,
"You cannot start the day on an empty stomach,
"Be quiet. Nobody asked you anything,
"Speak when spoken to,
"Mind your manners,
"When we go in this store, do not ask me for nothing,
And you better not have anything in your pockets
when
we leave here,
"Do not sit on cold porches or steps."
"Stop wearing wet socks."
"Stop all that running"
"Just pray about it"
"Jesus is listening to you all the time,"
This is only poem one.
So for now we are done.
Theirs is so much more and so there must be at least a
poem two.
That is what I have decided is best to do.

My Mom's Expressions

Mom's say things like,
"A little soap and water never killed anybody and
It won't harm you."
"You will know when your older.
"Don't rush growing up.
"Am I talking to a brick wall?
"I did the same things when I was your age.
"Are you going out dressed like that?
"I'm your mother not Ms. …..
"I brought you in the world and I will take
you out,
"Clean up after yourself,
"I am not your maid,
"You must think I was born yesterday,
"Are you mentally challenged or something?
"Do you think those clothes are gonna pick
their self up?
"If you show off, I will wear that but out right there
and not when we get home,
"Do you need a hearing aid?
"The little bird told me"
"You are going to church whether you
like it or not,
"Don't make me come in there,
"Go outside and play. It is a beautiful day.
"Where did you get that lying from?
"How many times do I have to tell you no,
"I do not have to explain myself. I said no,
"You are not my mother, I'm yours,
"Close your mouth before you catch flies,

"I do not buy food for the neighborhood,
"Don't embarrass the family,
"Why do I have to keep repeating myself. If
I said it once, I said it a thousand times,
"I'm not gonna ask you again,
"Look at me when I am talking to you.
"You are getting on my last nerve,
"If you put things where they belonged, you would
find them now wouldn't you,
"When I was you age…
"Stop stumping up those stairs,
"No running in the house,
You eat to much, I think you have a tape worm,
Pretty girls keep their clothes clean,
Young ladies cross their legs,
You better stick around and learn how to cook
something"
"Mommy loves you and so does daddy and Jesus,
Shut your eyes and you will go to sleep,
"Act like you have some common sense in your head"
"We are not like everybody else"
Pick that stuff up before someone falls and breaks their
neck,
And that's a wrap.
It will end with that.
This is not to say that there is not many left
Unsaid,
Such as turn the lights off and take your little but
to bed.

MY Dad's Expressions

"Your mother will take care of that one,

"What did I say? And don't you forget it,

"You must think that I'm your mother,

"I will skin you alive,

"And that's that,

"I will turn this car around,

"Be ready,

"I gave you all the money you are going to get,

"Do you need me to take some of it back?

"Sleep over? I need peace and quiet,

"When I say go to bed, I mean get in it,

"I work from sun up to sun down and then some,

'Ask your mother,

"I will give you something to cry about,

"Keep your elbows off the table,

"Stop being a cry baby,

"Your mother and I run this house,

"Fight until you are bloody,

"I didn't raise no cowards,

"Is that understood,

"Stand up straight and stop slouching,

"Take some responsibility,

"Act like you got some sense in your head,

"I will knock the daylights out of you.

"This is your mother's and my money,

When you are old enough to work, then

you will have your own,

"Do you think I am running a pig stein,

"As long as I put a roof over your head, food on the
table, shoes and clothes on your back,

"That is all that is required of me,

"If you need me, let me know,

And my dad always said,

"It is hotter than a Montana oven with the damper down,

"No sir,

"Where's your mother?

"Of course I love you, I'm taking care of you. That
In itself ought to tell you that,

What did I just say,

"You children are going to eat me out of house and
home,

"I will slow walk you down,

Nobody is going to date any of my daughters,

And,

You better bet,

Whatever dad said, dad met.

Who Was I

Who was I,
Was I my mother's son,
Was I the beloved,
hallowed born male
in my family,
My father's delight and yet,
There was born two,
But now tragically only
left to bring in the family
off spring only one,
Were my cries, my bemoans
for life,
For help,
 Below the moon that
pierced the dark velvet sky,
That aphotic, cryptic night,
Did they echo the cries that took
place way back when the slaves
cried and bewailed as they were drug to the
shores of no more?
Who was there to hear my cries of help?
Who was there for me as I let out my last
sighs as I died?
I lay on a cold slate three days like a
tossed away slave,
Cold, lifeless and alone,
Ignored, and tossed to the side
my phone,
Just long enough to cover up
any truth that might would
have come out,
Now framed and being blamed,
Disgrace being placed by my name,
I fought as hard as I could to live,
I tell you, I did,
I was ever so brave,
As on the grass I lay,
That night that I fought for my life
and my right to live and travel as I did,
I fought to be where I was,
I fought for the right to walk freely as me

under that beaming moonlight,
I fought for the right to be a dark skinned
man given the right to place a hood
of cover over my head because
of the cold and rain,
I fought for the right to embrace my family again,
But tragically,
A frightful, calamitous,
Insufferable, appalling,
gruesome, grim demise
would be my plight,
And now after all you have done,
You try to damage and further devalue
my lifeless being,
You want to squash who I was
like a bug under your foot with
no meaning,
But,
The heavens have intervened,
The world has told you no,
This is and was our son,
A human being,
Our brother,
A destined father,
His mother's and his dad's adored son,
Our beloved one,
Black,
White,
Hispanic,
And oh no we are not done,
From the highest office,
To the furthest part of the world,
Just about everyone,
They heard and hear the grief of a
Grieving mom and dad,
They hear my cries too finally
although I do not dwell any longer
under the sun but rest in the Son,
Justice for me is reigning,
As I rest with God's son.
We got you covered Trayvon Martin.

61

The Hoodie

You are soft and covering,
As I move, you provide,
Warmth,
Protection,
Style,
Privacy,
Covering,
Yes! Some have been infamous
under you,
That is true,
But,
not the majority I say,
No! Not the majority at all.
One way direction,
Forward, I press,
Sometimes simply breezing by the things I pass,
Destination without procrastination,
Snuggled under so tightly as I walk,
Run,
Stroll,

To cold to do without you,
Bold enough to speak about you,
You are worn in different styles from
culture to culture by any human,
This includes,
Young ins, woman, men,
How is it that for only one culture you
represent only danger, only sin?
Couldn't that sin apply to most anyone?
It is the behavior associated with it when done
that fuels the fear,
But,
Know that it is true for any culture, any time,
and anywhere.
And
Understand that this is
not the only selected choice and gear,
Folks do what they plan in the face that smiles,
With no covering at all,
Without any regard, respect, repentance or fear.

The Image I See

I look at a form in the mirror,
Cheval glass,
I behold the semblance,
Just because I do,
May mean quite nothing,
This I say and express,
This I share with you too,
Sometimes when I peer
at what appears reflected and
projected,
I see the most awesome image,
The best,
That fills me with such happiness,
That makes me full of joy,
That makes me giggle,
Like when you buy something
that makes you happy,
And it is of worth, value, precious, rare,
And it is of truth,
I surely, surely do,
But what do you do when the
Image appears void,
Glaring as if being hidden behind the
deepest gray cloud,
Almost out of view,
What should you do if the weight of the
load that you are carrying gives
you an obscure view,

Darkness that is the deepest black,
Not giving light,
So that the image beheld is
Diminutive,
Stunted,
a diminutive view,
What if the effigy seen is a facade,
One formulated,
Contrived,
A replication,
One that you gladly give accolades too,
But however,
This mental grasp,
Interpretation,
Perception,
Conjecture and illusion of view,
This image only exist with you,
Well,
The bible deals with having the
right image of one's self,
Within this wisdom lye the keys to
a true self-image,
The essence of attitudes,
The essence to a flourishing,
proper view of self and life,
The trueness of the real self,
The image that you should behold as God does and
adoringly views,

Genesis 1:27 ESV / 117 helpful votes
So God created man in his own image, in the image of God he created him; male and female he created them.

Genesis 1:31 Kjv
31And God saw ever thing that he had made, and, behold, it was very good. And the evening and the morning were the sixth day.

1 Corinthians 3:16 ESV / 46 helpful votes
Do you not know that you are God's temple and that God's Spirit dwells in you?

1 Peter 3:3-4 ESV / 242 helpful votes
Do not let your adorning be external—the braiding of hair and the putting on of gold jewelry, or the clothing you wear— but let your adorning be the hidden person of the heart with the imperishable beauty of a gentle and quiet spirit, which in God's sight is very precious.

Psalm 139:13-16 ESV / 109 helpful votes
For you formed my inward parts; you knitted me together in my mother's womb. I praise you, for I am fearfully and wonderfully made. Wonderful are your works; my soul knows it very well. My frame was not hidden from you, when I was being made in secret, intricately woven in the depths of the earth. Your eyes saw my unformed substance; in your book were written, every one of them, the days that were formed for me, when as yet there was none of them.

Although I may not possess striking
physical features of beauty,
This, I have found does not clearly
reflect all that is in the mirror,
All that I and others view,
Physical beauty can be beholding,
But complete beauty is more than
what can be beheld at glance or
two,
God ended with all that I made was good,
Wonderful,
Therefore,

Lack of confidence in self is tossed out,
Just remember if the image is not good,
It was from the beginning,
The embodiment of God himself,
And,
God can fix it all with His Holy word,
God will eradicate the useless image and
bring to fruition, a breviloquent image
that is gleaming and glowing with
transparent beauty,
Inside and out.

Tanka

Friends
Friends are just like seeds
planted along your life path,

You must tenderly,
You must truthfully love, care,
Then ever they will be there.

Epic

Hercules
Hercules was a hero that showed up
just in time. He was the strongest man
on earth and was considered very wise.

There was nobody that compared to his strength. For a
lot of folks he became
their sure defender against all evil doers. Against their
enemies and all willing to offend.

Father

Father
Male, Masculine
Caring, Guiding, Giving,
Provider, Worker, Protector, Financier,

Loving, Hugging, Tugging,
Stern, Wise,
Man

Cool Move

A cool move is
a move made when
you are unaware of an
insolent decision,
At least so it appears,
It is an act that is indifferent,
despicable and not nifty,
Not hunky-dory or kind,
It is made to disturb a naive heart,
Caught off guard by a frigid, apathetic,
offish, loathsome soul,
They implement,
Keen cruelness and un-commendable
acts,
Repulsive, repugnant, and non-copacetic,
Yet,
The caring decent beings acts are quite
different,

They are respectable, meritorious, laudable,
And just simply wonderful,
They are praise worthy,
Excellent,
Exquisite,
Masterly,
Duper,
Temperate,
And most of all on time,
You can choose to have any kind of character
that best represents who you are,
Just remember,
Pleasant, talented, caring, sensational,
personable, sophisticated personalities are most
pleasing.
Although often times it may appear to be the
hateful, shrewd and scheming.

If You Want
IMMITATE

If you want,
You can emulate, parody,
model my example,
If you want,
You can choose to do all I do too,
Some things happen to include:
Drinking and
Constant boozing,
Sinning and loosing,
Fighting and striking,
Back biting,
In stolen cars carousing,
Smoking and doping,
Discoing all the time and
dishing all responsibility,
Disrespecting and neglecting
to educate your mind,
And, choosing to hold bars
and do time,
Jiving and lying,
Compromising and jeopardizing,
Expiring and crying,
Conniving and despising,
Scheming and cheating,
Shaming and gaming,
Hating and mutilating,
Filthy acts and demeaning,
Constant plotting of attacks,
Shooting, stealing and looting,
Pimping and beating the female
counterpart to the ground,
Crude and shrewd,

Influencing others for evil,
Deceitful and a deceiver,
Lawless and Conscienceless,
Causing hurts and constant frowns,
loathing and raping,
Bullying and slaying,
Beyond misbehaving,
Misdeeds and sneaky,
Or,
You can do as I do too,
Learning and yearning,
Caring and sharing,
Responsible and reliable,
Dreaming and Believing,
Soaring and flying,
Encouraging and Supporting,
Creating and blessing,
Pursuing and achieving,
Smiling and gleaming,
Having vision and
Making good decisions,
Praying and no straying,
Dependable and enjoyable,
Obeying and sin forsaking,
Confessing and professing,
Yielded and shielded,
Anointed and appointed,
Enjoying a well-planned life that
Is rewarding and pleasing,
Even if there was,
Struggling, and striving,
Living but not dying.

67

HAPPINESS

Happiness is,
Cheerfulness,
Lightheartedness,
Liveliness,
Sunniness,
Restfulness,
Peacefulness,
Gladness,
Blissfulness,
Bless fullness,
Good spirits,
Good harmony,
Good feelings,
Good humor,
Good cheer,
Its,
Elation,
Enchantment,
Enthusiasm,

Ebullience,
Effervescence,
Exuberance,

Euphoria,

It is,

Peace of mind,

Pleasure,

Prosperity,

Positivisms,

Proper views,

It is the "Beatitude's"

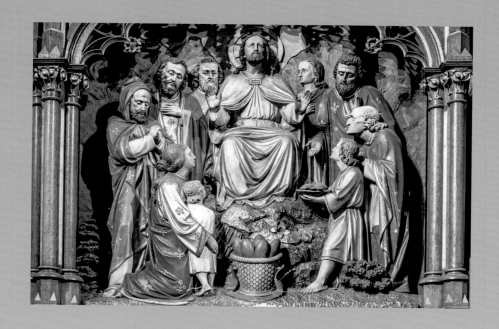

THE BEATITUDES

Gospel of St. Matthew 5:3-10
"Blessed are the poor in spirit,
for theirs is the kingdom of heaven.

Blessed are they who mourn,
for they shall be comforted.

Blessed are the meek,
for they shall inherit the earth.

Blessed are they who hunger and thirst for righteousness,
for they shall be satisfied.

Blessed are the merciful,
for they shall obtain mercy.

Blessed are the pure of heart,
for they shall see God.

Blessed are the peacemakers,
for they shall be called children of God.

Blessed are they who are persecuted for the sake of righteousness,
for theirs is the kingdom of heaven."

COMFORT

Comfort is,
Contentment,
Enjoyment,
Pleasure,
Realization,
Alleviation,
Assuagement,
Coziness,
Exhilaration,

Peacefulness,
How wonderful this life would be,
If all human beings focused on the comforting of others,
Going out of the way to be ever so kind,
Reaching out far and near to give out an abundance of love, peacefulness,
happiness and of course "Comfort",
The blessing that says I really, really care.

Sister

Sister
She, Female,
Nurturing, Protecting, Caring,
Influential, Factual, Relational, Exceptional,
Uplifting, Giving, Amazing,
Strong, Kind,
Sister

POSITIVE

renowned is noteworthy,
memorable is remarkable,
momentous is extraordinary,
prominent is well-known,
exceptionally taste like unusual,
particularly smells like strikingly,
eminent sounds like distinctly,

Acrostic
POET

I am a blessed poet,
Learning and gleaming from my own
constructed poetry,
Over a period of time
composing books,
Very inspired to write more styles,
Ever learning how to appreciate others gifts,

Putting forward my best efforts each time,
Two more books of poetry in mind so far,
Ending does not seem plausible,
Although likable,
Trying to say or forecast the future is hard,
Remembering to count my blessings nevertheless,
You are and will ever be the inspiration as to why.

ANAGRAMMATIC

Shower

How wonderful to do a soap splashing,
Why there is no way to estimate how long
the relaxing moments remain evident as thoughts
are flowing,

Soaking and laving just the same,
Scrubbing and cleansing toils, worries and soil away,
Even my surface cries for such sweet relief,
Oh how I await this lathering treat,
Reminiscing this relaxing and sensuous waste deep.

BOP

"Selfish Responses"

I can never figure out how selfishness
Is and has become such prevalent a
response to the asking of the
question of will you please do me
this favor that I really need your help
with ever so desperately.

How come in a society where we are
blessed more than ever before with
resources and the abundance of money

means, transportation, houses, lands,
clothing, and food and the list still goes
on and on because God has given us
so much and yet if we are asked to help
out we can readily say a point, blank no,

I think that people need to experience what
it is like to struggle for a bit or two if the
attitude is that they can easily ignore the
needs of their sisters and brothers with
no hesitation or feeling of guilt when
that there response will make the difference.

CASCADE

Purpose

We were put here in this world for purpose,
We were to make purposeful strides and mature,
We are to excel and create, and, evolve,
We are to cherish God most of all,

How does this confuse and traumatize the masses,
Why does the meditation of it cause such lamentation,
Is not it necessary to make inquisition, proposition,
We were put in this world for a purpose,

Screaming with cries of you just still remain, same,

Knowledge requisitions your void gray matter,
She says bluntly with disappointment, assimilate,
We were to make purposeful strides and mature,

Squeezing out moments as if there were none,
How dare you act as if you are perplexed,
Have you any intellect to bequeath, disseminate,
We are to excel and create, and evolve,

Shatter the notion of your dammed being,
Ignorant of divine purposes denoted by time,
Pandemonium is the response for mere intelligence,
We were put in this world for a purpose.

Sculpting

"The Seven"

I have already
                  P
                    U
                      B
                        L
                          I
                        S
                      E
                  D

Four other poetry books and
two short stories!

ELEGY

SO LONG

So now is the feeling of woe in the midst
of monstrosity that was contrived in delusion,
So how does the soul yet dare to own such a
violent fallacy,
Yet the occupancies of such matters continues
to claim her so longs,
So long to ya,

Never return, never ever again,
Abandon that mirage, virtual reality,
Sorrow nor pity belongs to you,
Only stupidity and arrogance,
Flee such spuriousness,
Void will be the encounter,
So long to ya,
Never ever return again, so long.

Fibonccia Concealed

Knowing
That there
Is more than
Just what the view portrays

Since the truth is evident and also eclipsed
because the ultimate incubation thoughts
encompassing infinite sources of
cryptic processes are concealed.

FUNDING

What if I had the money that I needed?

I might be able to accomplish my dreams,

What if someone cared to help with their funds?

I could become all that I desire and greet my destiny,

What if I could really accomplish these desires, these
dreams?

I would bless many others and help them accomplish
many things.

TRIBUTE

Dessert
This is just to say
I have eaten
The desserts
That were in the fridge,

And which you were probably

Saving
For snack,

Forgive me
They were scrumptious,
So delicious,
And so sacchariferous.

Sweet Dreams

"COWS"
Last night I dreamt about cows,
There were cows everywhere,
There were cows in my kitchen,
There were cows standing on chairs,
There were cows in my basement,
There were cows in my bedroom upstairs,
There were cows all around me mooing by my feet,
And disturbing my dreams while I tried to sleep,

They were in my bathroom and around my sink,
They were in the bathtub and one of them had a nose
with a ring and utters that were pink,
They were near my ears mooing and that filled
me with dread,
There were cows, cows, cows,
As far as I could see….
When I awoke today I noticed,
There was milk in a bucket beside my bed.

Being Someone Else

When you try to be
Someone else,
God will sit you down himself,
When you fix your attentions upon
who they are,
When you snarl, and bark at any thing
that they have accomplished successfully,
Honestly,
Triumphantly,
Dedicatedly,
That they have achieved with the help of God,
When you try to take their place,
You fake all their attributes,
Their talents,
Their abilities,
Their strides,
Their accomplishments,
And then talk about them you with misconceptions,
And horrendous lies,
Attack their very being while constantly scheming,
Then God himself will be their avenger,
God will intercede,
For you see,
Your heart is seething with envy, guile, vile filth,
Cruelty,
Bullying anger,
Disgraceful, violent acts unlike God,
But God will correct you,
"This please do not doubt!"
God will intercede,
When you try to surround them with violence,
When you try to surround them with filthy shame,
The things that you are made of,
Such shameful filth that is easy for you to practice
and live out,
They are not like yourself,
So please do remember,
God is their avenger,
He will help them out,
You protest their righteousness,
You are bitter and full murder and scheming,

Like Cain, and Pharaoh who kept trying to
Keep God's children in chains,
You manipulate and try to wickedly
influence those against them who love them,
Those who him or her they adore,
You want their name tarnished and banished,
You want to rid them of their
Accomplishments and blessings,
Their very life and all their goods,
No matter the suffering that you cause,
You simply continue,
Your heart is the heart of Satan,
Your master,
But please do not forget,
God is their avenger,
He will help them out,
God will intercede,
You are crude crud, no good,
Jesus made this clear in his scriptures,
He also told some vicious, angry,
Violent, hell bent folks off, all the time too,
You feel that they should be pulled
To the dyers straits, abyss, substratum part of life,
Especially if they are married and are
a clean, charming devoted, Godly
man, and a loving God obeying wife,
Please, remember,
God is their help,
God will intercede,
And so you launch your vicious plans
Carried out by your demonic followers,
Sometimes this is masterminded
Involving numerous people,
Holding esteem power on high levels,
And the effects and cruelness reaches
Seemingly endless boundaries,
It even entraps those who actually knew
nothing,
You constantly set traps,
You make it appear as though
You are repaying them back,

And that yes, they deserve whatever
all that you conjure,
Or,
Contrive according to your convoluted
non-truth premise of thoughts, and lies,
Yes, fascinating evil that makes
Folks stop and wonder, cry out to God,
You admire and look forward to and brag
about your own vicious tactics,
You constantly gleam and look for
approval to carry out your schemes,
Attacks,
You laugh outward and sneakily,
You plan consistently just like demons,
For you are possessed by them,
But your actions will reach God's heaven
above,
And,
Just when you think that you have gotten
Away with it all,
God will intercede,
You manipulate and try to wickedly
Influence those who help them,
You want them abandoned by all,
You want to possess their very soul,
You want to take away their name in marriage,
You want them addicted to substances,
You want them to be prostituted,
You want them ugly and nowhere near cute,
You want them without help and friends,
You want them without family,
Over them you want to violently reign,
You want to isolate them for your special

brand of violence,
And why,
Why?
Because you want their named stricken and
silenced,
And why again I say and ask again,
Because they have no need of you or your company,
You are not their choice of companionship,
And therefore you have launched a deadly
campaign to make their life a life of regret,
And fret,
All because they do not want your
Desired choices,
All because they do not want you,
But God,
But God sits high and looks below and is in control,
What violence you put out against them,
You and yours will reap it back as twice that,
So sniggle and giggle as you watch carried out
Plots and schemes,
Sniggle and giggle as you carry out what you
Planned, conceived,
What you schemed,
But then remember,
You are not in charge of anything,
When your life is called to death,
Then,
Suddenly,
Now you are expiring,
You came with no one's soul but your own,
You will exit and leave with nothing you gained
or own and only your dammed being.

Race

Stacy liked to race,
Up and down the school staircase,
She always walked with haste,

It did not matter the place to
race as long as you tied your shoe
laces and kept up with the pace.

PEPPER

Nothing is hotter than pepper,
Too much may leave a blister,
On the tongue or lips and yes,
This matters,
And pepper causes your thoughts to flutter,
It will turn you into a beggar and
Make you ask and beg for water,
Some do like it milder,

Some say the hotter the better,
So please sons and daughters,
If you do not want to be out of order,
Do not put too much in liquid cheddar,
Sauces, meats, veggies, and even now sweets,
Because that error will change your flavor,
And cause it to be extremely hotter,
And so with it you must be wiser.

NIBBLE

Crystal with the dimples liked to nibble
on pretzels,
And sometimes candy like
caramel,
Or for breakfast a bagel,
Or a cookie with icing in the middle,
And yet she is quite bashful,

And blushful,
And does a chuckle,
When syrup is poured on hot
Apple cereal and scrapple,
That makes her insides
happy and bubble with gleeful,
Thankful, cheerful sys.

Grey Clouds

When you see gray clouds,
Followed by thunder very loud,
Push your way through the

crowd to safety where you are
allowed.

HOLE

Now that you have found a black hole,
Fall down inside of it, craw, now go!
Never ever return ever again,
Stay there until your eternal end.

YOU ARE SNEAKY

Malicious, Cowardly, Shifty, Duplicitous,
You are double-dealing, deceitful, and surreptitious.

SLIME

You are contemptible, slippery, disingenuous, and imposturous,
Also misleading, cunning, deplorable, and treacherous.

Beguiling

Being roguish, misleading, indirect, and seeming,
Is being phony, serpentine, snide, insidious, and scheming.

Hoodwinking

To be disreputable, sordid, foul, traitorous, and sinuous,
Is being circuitous, sleazy, shabby, backbiting,
immature and unscrupulous.

PREVIEW

Have you gazed into those pupils
that appear to tell a story
far ahead,
Almost as if a glimpse into heaven,
A preview before the destination,
Have you noticed the energy floating
around this being?
And, more than Earth its self,
Angelic flutters, Angelic flutters,
Throughout, throughout,
A message screaming at you loudly,
But, still,
Quietly,
Calmly,
Lovingly,
Preoccupied by mundane business,
Yet,
Giving and creating I'll never forget
these moments,
Brazen and bold,
Yet, clueless to what may lie ahead,
Cunning is the evil one camouflaging dread,
Inclination saturated with potions of lure,
Apprehension far gone,
Blurry panorama and delayed introspection,
Hypothesis deceived,
Then a day of forever changing with combustion,
Takes place,
Transpires,
Nullification of dreams,
Everyone should know that the here and now
Will surely one day change,
Glimpses through peering ovals told the story,
They sure did,

Approximations, rearranged,
Floating on clouds of comfort,
Head resting in its forever place,
Smiles that cannot be replaced,
Until the pearly gates,
Only as a reminder to be kind and
appreciate those, family, and all,
who cross your path,
Walking hand in hand with Jesus some how
A heart does let you know,
A heart given from him from the very
start although,
Met with various woes,
And now,
A soul is never transitioning solo,
It is carried by those who send it
through with prayers, cares and yes tears,
It is greeted by heaven's host when
Jesus they do his will the most,
It is true that Jesus you must receive
before dining in his presence,
Remember his words clearly,
You are not to do the separating of souls
destinations,
I do that best,
I know the heart,
I know what I share last when a soul departs,
Weep not in vain,
But,
Live to live again,
When you truly love,
When you truly love,
You will live to live again!

I Thought Just For A Moment

I thought just for a moment,
A bit, a wink or two,
Ticking fleeting second of a breath,
What is the preciseness of the matter,
I tried to substantiate the relevance and the
magnitude of its corporeality,
Just simply for the moment,
Blasted is that zero,
Grievance with sterile perplexities,
Only God remains,
Dipping into borrowed eminence,
The creator at the beginning explains,
 All in vain,
All in vain,
Here,
Dwelling in the sum of substance,
Not just for a moment,
But a mere point in the interval,
Retrospectively,
I found that Rhythmical seasons,
For me, was and is the cruelest temporal core,
Nucleus of the burdens that be,
Eternal life or death,
A moment bound to be,
It never stayed long enough to convince me of
Its favor,
That death moment thing,
So I chose unfruitful moments to let flee,
Duration of moments are welcomed when the
Interludes and phenomenon grants comeuppance,
Even if just for a moment,
Twirling like a flavored lollipop vibrant,
You've seen,

Do not however, get caught up in the spin of no end,
Unless it is quite notable, with usefulness spins,
Never is it though,
The harshness of reality will knock you down and cause
You to spin,
For more than a moment,
For more than a moment friend,
A mere meager, irrelevant attitude toward
A denotation moment or moments has
preoccupied your existence,
Thunderous, calamitous, grieving, droppings
Of furry is your response,
But really it is mountains of pure bullshit,
Hidden in what you perceive to be sophisticated,
undetectable garbage, and the more you pile,
The deranged factor explodes,
Pitiful is the creator's response, just pitiful,
And,
You always reject every phenomenal gift sent that
You cannot control,
However,
You evolve according to the piles of garbage put
In your pathway to maneuver around anyway,
Nothing but ejectamenta, excrement, stupefied
manure from those with putrefied, foul minds,
Surely they too neglected to read Solomon,
Now,
Butterflies are not controlled,
They flutter about freely while creating
moments of wonder and intense joy
when they burst on the scene,
I think I will fly with the butterflies,
If only for moments.

81

All Is Vanity

1 The words of the Preacher,[a] the son of David, king in Jerusalem.

2 Vanity[b] of vanities, says the Preacher,
 vanity of vanities! All is vanity.
3 What does man gain by all the toil
 at which he toils under the sun?
4 A generation goes, and a generation comes,
 but the earth remains forever.
5 The sun rises, and the sun goes down,
 and hastens[c] to the place where it rises.
6 The wind blows to the south
 and goes around to the north;
around and around goes the wind,
 and on its circuits the wind returns.
7 All streams run to the sea,
 but the sea is not full;
to the place where the streams flow,
 there they flow again.
8 All things are full of weariness;
 a man cannot utter it;
the eye is not satisfied with seeing,
 nor the ear filled with hearing.
9 What has been is what will be,
 and what has been done is what will be done,
 and there is nothing new under the sun.
10 Is there a thing of which it is said,

"See, this is new"?
It has been already
 in the ages before us.
11 There is no remembrance of former things,[d]
 nor will there be any remembrance
of later things[e] yet to be
 among those who come after.

The Vanity of Wisdom

12 I the Preacher have been king over Israel in Jerusalem. 13 And I applied my heart[f] to seek and to search out by wisdom all that is done under heaven. It is an unhappy business that God has given to the children of man to be busy with. 14 I have seen everything that is done under the sun, and behold, all is vanity[g] and a striving after wind.[h]

15 What is crooked cannot be made straight,
 and what is lacking cannot be counted.

16 I said in my heart, "I have acquired great wisdom, surpassing all who were over Jerusalem before me, and my heart has had great experience of wisdom and knowledge." 17 And I applied my heart to know wisdom and to know madness and folly. I perceived that this also is but a striving after wind.

18 For in much wisdom is much vexation,
 and he who increases knowledge increases sorrow.

Abstract

WOE
Gloom is doom,
Grown is gone,
discreet is fleeting,

Sneaky is creepy,
Dishonesty taste like vanity,
Fairness smells like blessings,
Cunning sounds like deceit.

SEASON
THOSE SEASONS

Spring is buzzing, blooming, birthing,
Summer is chirping, splashing, flashing,
Autumn is turning, cooling, falling,
Winter is, freezing, blistering, numbing.

RHETORICAL BIRDS

I wonder if they like being birds?
I suppose they do,
They always like flying high in the sky and soaring over roof tops,
They never stay on the ground and they only come down there to eat,
Some people say that they wish that they could fly like birds too,
Birds make life very exciting, interesting, wonderful, cool and that my
friend, at least for me, is definitely true.

Octopoem
Buzzers

Covered with yellow and black,
Hungry for summer flower nectar,
Flying in peoples yards about,
Gleaming in the sunny warm season,
When it rains, it buzzes its way to a surface and
continuously protects itself with its furry coat,
It anchors its legs like a strong table against the weather,
Survivor,
Thriving at the nectar buffet.

SEASONS

Snow
The snow twirls down to the earth like floating feathers,
And sometimes the motion of it is very fast and clever,
It takes its time and builds a white, glistening, beautiful blanket,
That covers every object, building, and tree as far as the eye can see,
It does this by sitting still wherever it lands unless moved by : the wind, melted by
rain or mist, nature and animals, or moved and scattered by any human being activity,
It is stored in the clouds all summer, autumn, fall and spring,
And it leaves tearfully as it freezes and unfreezes and then melts continuously.

If Were
"PEACE"

If peace were a color it would be pastel green,
Flowing from land to land and bordering every
ocean, river, pond, sea and stream,
It would grow new wisdom, new joy, new love,
new acceptance, peace and new dreams,
New harmony and new patience that grows as tall as
trees,
If peace could be a taste it would be fresh baked bread,
It would smell and taste so wonderful until you would
abandon all violence, terror justification dread, war
and then sit at a table and break bread together instead,
If peace could be a smell it would be the smell of fresh
blooming flowers,
That gives off a pleasant scent and this scent renews
itself every hour,
It would be that way no matter the season, always
fragrantly pleasing,
And because the smell was so pleasant, no one would
have thoughts of being mean, but only love and respect
for every human being,
If peace were a sound, it would be a bell that rang
every morning and in the evening again as well,
It would ring for harmony, It would ring a beautiful
melody,
It would ring because it was time to worship God,
It would ring to celebrate each brand new blessed
morning and then praises to celebrate a gracious day
just ending,
It would ring to remind us to love, to be kind, to
end and

start each day with praise and prayer,
If peace were a feeling it would be a warm blanket,
To comfort those being born in to the world day or
night,
It would warm up men's hearts and compel them to
care,
It would bring warmth and friendship to God's
children under
the sun everywhere and then there would be no longer
any war to fear,
If peace were an animal it would be a gracious lion,
It would roar for the strength of reverence that we had
for all mankind,
It would roar for the honor and respect taught to the
small and then roar for the elders setting the right
examples for them all,
It would roar for the mothers who bent their knees to
God in prayer,
It would roar for the fathers who were at the head of
every family leading and providing,
Guiding, protecting, rearing and raising the young
correctly everywhere,
It would roar to celebrate all nations full of the
blessings and the favor of God across their lands,
It would roar out the worship of God daily, Jehova,
Jesus, The Lord God Almighty, The Master, The Savior
Of Mankind,
The Roaring mighty King!

Limmerick
NOG

There once was a frog named nog,
Who ate flies until he was groggy,
But the flies didn't mind to be treated so unkind,
They were just glad to keep him full and busy.

Lament

JOY
I am joy,
I dress in the colors of luminous white and yellow,
I need only more hearts to brighten and paths to lighten,
I am related to happiness and peace and we travel together
no matter the circumstance, no matter the heart in the human being,
I vacation in love and it is my resting place, I revive
folks daily,
And I help keep bitterness out of hearts and on folks faces,
My job is simple and that is to keep joy ever flowing and growing,
To help people understand that joy is what they should be showing always and be sowing,
I desire that people everywhere would spread more joy and cheer,
To be joyous as much as possible,
To love always and care.

Verb Verse

Movement

Arrive, appear, attend,
Announce, call, connect,
I will be awaiting your entrance.

Numbers

Add, balance, calculate,
Analyze, count, check,
I must arrive at the correct total.

NOTABLE

Admire, applaud, cheer,
Enjoy, notice, note,
You really stand out.

BRING

Supply, deliver, provide,
Carry, tote, gather,
The package will arrive soon.

POEM THAT YOU

This is the poem that penetrates the heart,
The mind, and the soul,
That awakens your inner being to
saturate itself with streams of intense, pure,
alleviating and unfolding love that heals the thoughts
and emotions,
Because all during the day's journey, someone may
have damaged, shattered precious feelings without
regard, without care,
Because maybe they in anger hurt you and you may
also
have been treated unjustly, unkind, un-forgiven and
unfair,
And when you awake crying and the tears cover your
face,
And you feel a bit of fear, distress, disgrace,
And when soothing rivers of comfort and forgiveness
bring healing waters that do and will appear,
Removing the heartache, despondency, desolation,
dejection

and drying away of all tears,
This is the poem that greets you there with words of
Consolation, lenity, assuagement,
Saying that it will be alright and do not fear,
That no matter how rough the day was, and indeed
it was,
It is done and now healing has begun and acceptance,
Is your deliverance,
So cheer up,
Things will be better and oh how the victory you will
proclaim,
When those hard moments are only a memory, an
anamnesis, and you are
flourishing again,
And when the lessons from them are cultivated,
accomplished and known,
And better opportunities will and have already begun,
We will find you anew again.
In harmony with yourself and God above.

I once knew

Odd Girl
I once knew a girl as odd as she could be,
She liked to eat peanut butter and mayo sandwiches,

And succotash and peas and mud pie,
And she didn't like chicken and French fries.

I Asked
NATURE

I asked the sky why wasn't its color blue today,
And then it let out an obstreperous, vociferant cry,
And then the gray clouds spiraled, and furled, as they bowed
and rolled away,
And in the midst of veering and swerving the color crystal
blue arrayed,
I asked the sun why was it hiding behind inflated,
floating, clouds,
Suddenly it rose up and stretched forth it's immense,
astronomical,
bright sunrays that lit up the earth and sent all
tenebrosity, obscureness,
every bit of cloudiness away,
I asked the flowers why haven't their efflorescence,
their awe flowering
presentation and even the opening of their buds
emerging, are not on
floweret display,
With blooming flowers yet to be in array, and some
appearing as perennial,
And then they began blooming on every stem and they
burst forth in unison as they peeled back their petals,
their petioles wide open and spread,
I asked the grass why wasn't it swaying, oscillating with
the wind,

And then it began to sway, oscillate back and forth and
then it stopped and then stood up straight,
And then, back and forth again,
I asked the birds why weren't they flying and tweeting
overhead today,
And then they began to sing in harmony while flying
as they did spins and twirls,
And then they all landed back in their nest as they
soared pass my head,
I asked myself what was wrong and should I be feeling
happy right now and not
dread and sad,
And then I looked at my God given view that peered
through God given sight,
And then the sun brightened, emblazoned, dressed up
the earth,
while a soft wind blew,
I found a place to ensconce down on the grass,
I sat there very quiet,
I began gazing, and peering up at the sky,
Gradually a feeling of calmness, tranquility, peace and
neutrality prevailed,
All was simply perfect,
So I lifted up my voice with praise to God who gave
me the opportunity to behold
what beautiful scenery and abundance of blessings that
He daily provides.

HOLD ON
FORWARD

Hold on to your faith and belief,
Even when everyone's around you
Is crumbling,
Hold on to respect for others,
Even when it is popular not to do so,
Hold on to your dreams,
Even when they appear to be fleeting,
Hold on to your friends,
Even when they get on your last nerve,

Hold on to your reverence for God,
Even when you are rejected by others,
Hold on to inspiration,
It will energize you when needed,
Hold on to reality,
Even when others have abandoned it,
Hold on to treasure and value your life,
It is the only one you get until you go to heaven.

Pantoum
SAVAGES

The demoniac, savage, maddened, vicious abased thugs,
Attacked, invaded, and ventured to exert control,
A putrid, grimy, loathsome, squalid, repulsive, nut,
Was demoralized, bastardized, subdued in its fecal,

Attacked, invaded, and ventured to exert control,
Crummy, sooty, slimy, depraved, foul, base and vile,
Was demoralized, bastardized, subdued in its fecal,
The repugnant, perverted, dirty, nefarious, ignoble rats,

Crummy, sooty, slimy, depraved, foul, base and vile,
A putrid, grimy, loathsome, squalid, repulsive, nut,
The repugnant, perverted, dirty, nefarious, ignoble rats,
The demoniac, savage, maddened, vicious, abased thugs,

THE MESSAGE

There was a messenger sent to earth,
A proclamation was made concerning his birth,
He came from Heaven's throne above,
He brought the message of freedom,
He first brought down to human kind the message of love,
The revelation, a revelation,
He stood for and brought mankind eternal freedom,
He set enslaved man free from his sins,
He set him free from the sin yokes that bound him from within,
He demonstrated how to suffer, suffer in love,
How to rise above torture, humiliation and even death,
To know what to treasure deep in his heart,
To be upright and contrite,
A nonviolent fight that took his life,
Crucified but risen, the Savior of righteous light,
Those who followed his freedom message,
Were crucified, dehumanized and yes too they also died,
This message of eternal freedom, this memorandum of eternal love,
Still, the message prevailed,
Still the message prevails,
Although all of mankind did not embrace this ordinance,
It did not stop this message and it never will,
There was another messenger born to earth,
No proclamation was made concerning his birth,
He brought the message of freedom,
He brought the message of love,
The revelation, a revelation,
He demonstrated what it is like to suffer trying
to change cruel, soul rooted hatred, biases, racism, bigotry,
intolerance, discrimination and partiality,
He promulgated rights for all those enslaved by the
yoke of injustice, unfairness and out right wrong,
Whether near or far, whether weak or strong,
He was a crusader for:
The right to vote no matter your race, or
color of your skin or face,
The right to eat in any restaurant and sit in there any where
with your sisters and your brothers no matter their color,
No matter their race,
Without sectarianism, Jim Crowism, or dogmatism,
The right to socialize with any race and yet not jeopardize your safety,
No sexism, narrow mindedness, or racialism,
The right as a woman to be treated as an equal,
Not to be raped by any man kind or treated harsh and cruelly,
The economic right of the woman to bring home a pay,
And not have to clean houses and cook only for her wages,
Not exploited, brutalized, or exist as a sex slave,
Not to be happy to be considered and called a maid,
No chauvinism, antipathy, or dishonesty but equality,
Not owned but honored,
Appreciated, uplifted, supported and loved,
The right as a man when applying for a position,
Not to be considered lastly or not at all,
Or to be looked at as if they have a color condition,
The right to be a part of a flourishing economic society,
The right to offer their children afforded privileges,
The right to offer them in life good choices, a variety,
The right to be educated and elevated,
The right to earn fair wages and perform on any stage and stages,
The right not to be hauled and locked up because of skin
tones that reflect hues from tan to dark or darker than a raisin,
The right not to be overlooked for promotions and then called lazy,
The right to live beside any race of neighbor and not to be trapped in
underprivileged neighborhoods,
This nonviolent fight that took his life,
Was a push for justice, and push for equal rights,

The messages of the two ministers also proclaimed the right to exist safely,
The right to be treated as a woman and the right to be treated as a man,
The right to be treated as a human being and never, ever some ones
Dog,
And so the message still exists and is still being promulgated,
Those who crusaded, and believed Martin's freedom message of rights,
Were traumatized, dehumanized, brutalized and tortured paving the way for me
and yes, you too,
And although certain changes good and best for all have now
taken center stage and prevailed,
The struggle still continues, a struggle of will,
This message of overcoming brought the changes necessary for mankind,
It elevated the masses and brought about better wages and earnings,
Opportunities, and afforded rights too for us all,
But in this mist of this forward dream achieving generation,
Grievous atrocities and new problems still and do exist,
There is the realization that although we are overcoming and ascending,
And no longer are pushed or shot down in streets by cops,
Sprayed down by the water hydrogen,
Or chased by dogs,

And beat by bully pins,
Or locked up because of the color of your skin,
Or did I just over look what is still happening,
Young black men and women still suffer violently the treatment of police,
And as well as from each other, yes sadly, each other,
Black youth are pushed, kicked and killed daily across the nations in the streets,
They are chased by dogs and beat with bully pins,
Subject to random stopping and incarcerated disproportionately in a system
created to keep and entrap them forever with in,
Modern slavery, now legal again,
This modern day slavery prevails again with help sadly from our own race, because of intolerance,
History repeated all over again, and again, and again,
The Black Youth's life is not worth anything,
We call them kings and they are still seen as nonhuman,
Nonbeings,
Yes, some have escaped but not hardly enough,
Most treated harshly, killed instantly, or simply tossed like trash,
Written off as thugs,
Worst of all He hates himself, his wife, his children and others,
Those who do not receive the message of freedom and love,
The struggle wears him out, and so now he resides to becoming a drug
Lord,
The woman is raped and her baby is a blob,

In order to provide for her family she works two jobs,
She is raped by everyone including other women now,
How awful,
Nobody wants to obey God's word, let alone read it,
You know, that century best seller book called "The
Bible"
The young and the older man of any race,
Sometimes she can barely lift her head because of the
disgrace,
The children aren't taught and in school they aren't
learning,
They are strung out on calming pills and will do most
anything
violent,
Worst, they fail to learn survival skills,
However, because of love, grace and mercy some do
escape
the perils of life and reach back to any and to all still in
the struggle,
Maintaining in the fight, striving with all their might,
Yes, the black race indeed has prospered,
They have their own businesses,
Are educated,
Live and go as they please,
Women have rights and do also pursue their dreams,
However, in the midst of it all is still the same message,
When it is not blocked out,
It changes every situation.
Let us stop being hypocrites,

Stop the degrading,
Stop the enslaving and supporting rape,
We say it is prostitution and you know that it is a lie,
It is Human Trafficking not even and no longer
disguised,
Physically and mentally to both men and women,
Bringing shame and disgrace,
Stop finding a reason to be inhumane and cruel,
Unforgiving and untruthful,
Cunning and shrewd,
Jesus died loving us and Martin too,
The message is still the same,
Overcome, Overcome, when will all over come,
Oh freedom, Oh freedom over me, over me,
And before I be a slave, I'll be resting in my grave,
And go home to my Jesus and be free,
Has the reality,
The absoluteness and certainty of the message and
epistle,
The corporeality, totality, it's solidity and substance
reached you?
Penetrated your hearts, mind, soul, and total being,
Bringing about the needed changes,
For it is not a hypothesis, just an idea or neither
abstract in its conception,
It is sensible, tangible, authentic, genuine and true for
people of skin tones reflecting various hues,
Best for all,
And now you must choose.

Sonnet
THE DANCE

The shimmy took place in a dark space and lit,
The atmosphere appropriate, and central,
Filing in with no sequence it seems, did it,
Preparations simply perfect at best, goal,

Dedication, annunciation, foretold,
Splendid was the nourishment, refreshments, yum,
An oldest tried being youngish, response cold,
The young, energetic, curious, and much fun,

The festive occasion turned out amazing,
Shindig a big hit, birthday surprise was this,
Hub nob was the mingle theme besides dancing,
Was reserved, but DJ was reminiscing,
Danced like I did when I was a kid at shindig,
Danced until clothes soiled, do tossed, lights on,
best gig,

Etherege
The Growth

Pain,
Malady, affliction,
Attacked my side,
It swelled up like
A tennis ball with hollow
Liquid floating within and it was
Extremely agonizing, excruciatingly sore, afflictive, and vexing,
Awful, dire, urgent, serious, aching, dreadful, tender, inflamed,
Went to doctor, nurse, clinic, hospital three times crying,
Finally, one day it subsided inside on its own, glory!

94

Decuain
DECISIONS

Dear Heart,
When you make decisions, be thoughtful first,
Avoid corrupt choices, voices, options,
Do not give ultimatums, threats, cull hurts,
Prayer, meditation brings resolutions,
Righteous options, will bring solutions vague,
Be not known for arrogance, violence, war,
The wise spieler finds favor, coaction,
Wisdom ignites help, coalition.

TYBURN

The Plane
Whitest,
Brightest,
Politest,

Lightest,
Flying in the brightest, whitest, clouds,
The politest, lightest white plane soared!

The Ghoul

Blackness,
Heartless,
Weirdness,

Shortness,
Out of the blackness, appeared heartless
And with shortness and weirdness a ghoul!

The Active Bird

Tweeting,
Chirping,
Flapping,

Flying,
Tweeting in the nest and chirping was
The flapping bird while flying about.

Folks

Brighter,
Nicer,
Wiser,

Finer,
The nicer, kinder, and wiser folks
have brighter smiles and finer rewards.

The Bird

Rolling,
Moaning,
Roaming,

Floating,
Rolling down the hill moaning came the
roaming bird falling and floating in water.

Gleams

Wisdom is expressed
When choices are presented
And the right one gleams.

Exercise

Exercises seems
To be quite the challenge when
You do not just focus.

Diamante

THE FLOWER

Flower
Fragrant, Delicate
Growing, budding, spreading,
Colorful, yields, sprouts, buds,
Blooming, yielding, beautifying,
Seasonal, Germinating,
Plant

THE CAR

Car
Transporter, Carrier,
Rolling, Moving, Towing,
Automobile, Cart, Vehicle, Auto
Racing, Coasting, Cruising,
Vehicle, Cart,
Mobile

Rhyme
MINI

Mini got caught playing miniature golf
when she aught to have brought a book

and sought words for thought but now
she is distraught and her guilt she fought.

RHETORICAL

Flowers
I wonder if they like being flowers?
I suppose they do,
They always bloom in abundance,
They never fail to bloom from season to season,
Some people say that it is a good thing that God made
flowers to bring great

beauty to His earth,
Especially since they are filled with so many wonderful
fragrant smells,
they burst forth with delicate colorful petals yielding
toward the sunlight,
They make everything beautiful and fragrant.

FISH

I wonder if they like being fish?
I suppose they do,
They always like swimming in water deep and
shallow too,
They never stop swimming from shore to shore,
Some people say that they wish that they could be a
fish and
swim from ocean to ocean and sea to sea,
 I use to want to be a mermaid because when I was a
little one

I thought that they were real,
I no longer want to be a mermaid or fish of any type,
I do love to eat fish though,
They make aquariums beautiful and the oceans and
ponds and seas too,
Especially in the bright sun light,
They also make good food when eating them with any
dish you choose,
However, I'm sure that this they do not like.

IF Clouds

I wonder if they like being clouds?
I suppose they do.
They always appear in the sky and come down to
the earth as fog, rain, dew,
Sleet, and snow too,
They have different appearances and names called:
picture clouds, cumulous, stratus, cirrus, and nimbus
clouds,
They give glorious picture shows,
Whether the sky is grey, or beaming blue,
They are never the same whenever you see them in
view,

Although they have a distinguishable, similar form
that helps
Identify and gives them their names,
They make the sky very interesting and worth
peering at
when grey and furious right before a storm,
Telling you to take shelter to escape any harm,
But comforting, calming, too,
Like the feather cloud, cirrus, seemingly ready to
tickle you.

CARPE DIEM
Being A Blessing

"That sun just came blasting through the blueness of sky like a brand new pair of shiny shoes sparkling on display!" What a burst of energy. You know, how wonderful to start each brand new day with a burst of bright sunshine. Each dewy new morning is a pleasant fresh experience given to you to make whatever your heart and mind set to accomplish before it is done. Yes there are some challenges left over from yesterday but yesterday is now antiquated and tomorrow is filled with expectations of better. "Love God!" Humble your attitude. Search for ones to help or at least someone to uplift and when you have accomplish this for them, reach out for the next one in need of your generosity the most indeed. We can help those who really do not need us but that is not helping. "That is just having something do. So, "Live to love and give each day!" Take advantage of really living by giving and making a difference until you are reaching out your hands to Jesus and then now He will fill it with more than you can ever imagine!

Hold On Memories

old on too kind memories when
people were so wonderful to you,
You will need them when folks often try
too and do treat you very ferocious, cruel,
Hold on to your accomplishments,
Achievements, prized moments,
And display your degrees, diploma's and
certificates as a reminder to all that God
blessed you to be and have what you have,
He chose to give to you the ability to achieve,
You will need them when they try to discredit you,
Every degree, and all certificates,
They may mock you, try and degrade you,
Violently and viciously attack your being,
And want only to bend your head in utter shame,
Defame you and want and try to render you insane,
As if you have no sense,
Even when it is cumbersome to get up
out of the bed because of what has
been done and said,
Hold on to your smile and the giggles,
As you remember the situations that had you
chuckling, and cackling as your smile
was spread across your face,
Even when you have packed your smile away
because it hurts so much and you vowed
never to smile ever again,
Just hold on because,
You have so much, too much to give!

COLOR POEM PURPLE

This the color purple poem,
The color is purple,
Egg Plant is purple,
And so is a plum,
Grapes and turnips and,
I am still not done,
There is grape jelly and
That's purple too,
There are the flowers iris,
Amethyst, and lilac to
name a few,
Sea urchin,
Iris and lilac feels like purple,
There is purple foods like purple
Cabbage and potatoes and purple
Onions who knew,
And by the way, the words
Curdle, girdle, burble, gurgle,

Kerble, birkle, gergel, percle,
Pirkle, berkle, birkel, birtle, burkel,
Burkle, pirkle, purtle,
Terkel, terkle, turtle, all sound like
Purple, and so lets end this
purple poem with a
Tongue twister very soon,
Mr. turtle's name was
Burkle, birtle, burkle, birkle, berkle, burble,
And his cousin's name was,
Percle,pirkle, purtle,
And he named his daughter,
Gergle,gurgle, girdle,
And she named her doll kerble,
And her two birds,
Terkle, and Terkel,
And now we are through!

RHYME

The Hat

Mr. Jack,
Picked up a hat,

In the hat store at 2 o'clock,
Two hours before 4,
He then took it back,
Because it was too small.

Molly

Little Molly reached for
A good book to read from
the book shelf in her bedroom
beside her bed,
This is what she did,
Then she drank a glass of juice,
And,

Ate a cookie snack and not
Peanut butter and jelly on
bread,
 Reading a good
story instead of exercising was
her choice last night before
she went to bed.

HOLIDAY

Christmas
Christmas is a time of year
Where you see most folks
Giving,
Hearts are more loving
And ready for mending,
People tend to be way more friendly,
The cakes and deserts are the aromas
You see and taste from house to house
And place to place,

There are family and friend dinners,
Along with numerous celebrations,
And greetings of Merry Christmas too,
And when you meet and greet,
Folks will give you a warm embrace,
You hear the Christmas bells and the
Christmas carolers up until January 1st,
It is Jesus birthday, our Lord and Savior,
It is the most joyous time of the year!
It's Christmas!

I AM

I See And I Am
I am witty and charming,
And saved by God's Amazing grace,
So, for me,
I wonder why folks consider
Salvation alarming,
I hear heavenly music sometimes
When I awake in the morning,
And I see the intelligent side of God in all
creation,
How does this bring discomfort to any
human being,
I want peace, love, and forgiveness a
daily practice for all, starting with me,
Placidity, perseverance, pursuing of dreams,
I pretend that the world is perfect, and
that no one is unhappy about anyone or
anything,
I feel that more tranquility is in dire need,
So touch hearts I pray, and care about
their needs,
Then do what I can financially,
As God leads,
I worry that enough people do not have
Compassion, peace,
Care, and endow one another,
But spend day and night scheming,
And that far too many folks are mean,
And that too many people are bullies,
And that folks will kill you or do most

anything inhumane and cruel to any human
being,
I worry especially because they are
comfortable instead of being alarmed,
disheartened about these things,
I cry when I see the indifference, hate,
bias, and prejudices toward humans paraded,
accepted and celebrated,
An orgy of violence,
Blood thirsty demonic wickedness,
I am comforted when any act of kindness
is extended to those who really
need this and daily it should always be,
I understand that I am only one human being,
And that although the loving difference
I try to make may be so small,
I still believe the world changes for the
better one by one until we reach all,
I hope to inspire the masses to love,
care and positively change,
I am the first in my world that surrounds me,
But everyone should reach out and be the first
In their world too because it starts with you,
Do not wait for someone else,
An excuse,
Or better plan,
Just begin to be the blessing wherever you
abide,
As far as you are able too cross and reach the world,
Across this great big land.

THE POEM

A Poem
I can't write a poem right now,
Just forget it!
Because:
I am eating a pickle,
I am reading a book,
I have to go to the store,
I am folding my clothes,
I am raking the yard,
I am taking a shower,

I am vacuuming the floor,
I am taking a nap,
I am baking a cake,
I am riding my bike,
What?
The time to write one is up?
Uh oh!
Well all I have is this list of dumb excuses.
You like it? Really? No kidding.
Thanks a lot! Would you like to see another?

UNDERSTAND

Eternity
I do not understand,
Why males hurt females when they
like them and can't get their attention,
Why they will harm them dreadfully
Just to get some satisfaction,
Why after they truly, cruelly do them in,
They have the nerve to hang around
And then think their affections they will win,
But most of all what puzzles me is how folks
believe that there is a hell but not heaven,
Why they acknowledge and know that evil
exist and that a place of torment is what you

will and must face as your dwelling place at
the end,
To pay eternally for all those dreadful sins but not a
Beautiful eternity for the good called heaven,
What I understand most is that you
must believe in Jesus in norder to
attend and dwell in heaven at your end,
And that Jesus pardons all who ask for
forgiveness of all their sins,
And that you do not have to be perfect
to dwell and live there,
to get in.

USE TO JUST ME

I use to play with paper dolls,
But now I just love to learn about
fashion,
I always say my grace before I eat,
But I never eat succotash with green beans,
Or turnips or red beats,
I once went to the aquarium and saw such
beautiful fish,
But now I know after doing this that it takes
A lot of money to keep such a place in existence,
If I could I would have a museum and place
all the things God allowed me to create on view
for all to see,
I would charge not that much and have a place
to sit outdoors for those who wanted there to
eat their lunch and relax their minds freely,
I never stop dreaming and believing that wonderful
miracles do happen all the time,
But I might get discouraged when it appears
as if it takes so much or too much time,
Hopefully life will blossom wonderful despite
it all just fine,
I can't do some things sooner because of the lack
of funding,
But I can try little by little still to accomplish all
my goals one by one,
I won't be the only one ever to want to accomplish
such things,
But I might not see this come to pass,
Oh how I wish the opposite for me,
I use to dream and I still do,
And now, I have seen,
Some of my dreams come true,
But now I am simply striving and hoping that I am
allowed to accomplish each and every one of my
dreams and endeavors,
How about you?

IF

If Love
If love were a color,
It would be pastel pink,
As soft as a hand full of cotton,
Made into a warm fluffy quilt where
Underneath of it I would snuggle and
sleep,
And,
As tasteful as marshmallows before
And after melted,
It would be just like a new bright, fragrant,
Sunny day,
With a soft wind blowing,
And streams flowing,
With sparkles from the sun's rays upon
them as they flow or in still as
they lay,
If it were an emotion and it is, I would
keep it for all those who lacked it in
a bag of feathers,
So that I could blow it upon them as they
relaxed in nice breezy weather,
It would be available as soon as a second
from now,
The cost to have it, your heart,
In exchange for no more reason for
tears or frowns,
It would smell like the softest, alluring
perfume,
The scent would always linger from
Heart to heart,
It would never allow any foul odors

of harshness or break ups or doom,
It would be the endless moments that
leave you only never, or ever wanting it
to end,
And then stay there always,
Always caring and being more than a friend,
If it were a sound,
It would be the like a river,
Falling down a water fall,
Alluring and inviting,
Calling,
"Come here and stand under me!"
"There is plenty of room for all!"
"Come and experience the water as it flows
And pours on your body and face,"
And,
"Then take a drink of me to nourish your
entire being deep within,"
Alleviating you of all pain, heart ache, disgrace,
Love would be and do all God ever intended,
Never ending always,
For everyone to be in his love and daily in His
presence,
Forever, In God's loving presence where you simply
would
abide and
stay,
Of course, now that place is called the "New Paradise"
"Heaven,"
The eternal kingdom of never ending love, God's favor
and grace.

Epigram

Pants
I do not think me smart,
Or even know so much,
But even a dummy would
Know,
That those pant's need ironing
and starch.

Blues

If you do not comprehend that
"The blues" is not a color but
an emotion,
Then why with you carry on a
Conversation.

Similes

You are as jumpy as a kangaroo.
You are just as snappy like a gator.
You are just soft as and like flower petals.
You are as helpful as toilet paper.

You are as sparkly as diamonds.
Your movement is as quick as and like a tornado.
You cook like as if you were a chef.
You live elegant as and like a princess.

Metaphor

You are a song book that has endless songs.
You are my favorite dessert that I always consume.
Your words are lemony sour.
You are brown like tea in complexion.
You are strong like steel.
You are fragile like thin ice.

You are threatening like a bear.
You are clingy like used softener sheets.
You are beautiful and graceful like twirling snowflakes.
You are hungry like baby birds screaming for their meal.

Irony

You are as fast as a worm.
You are delightful as bitter coffee.
You are as gentle as sandpaper.
You are pretty like a weed plant.
You are slim like a hippo.

You are quiet like thunder.
You are peaceful like earthquakes.
You are harmless like tsunamis.
You are pleasant like acid.
You are cool like sun rays.

Analogy Poem

Fruit
Life is like a bowl of fruit,
Some of the fruit in the bowl
You may like, and some you may
 not,
Some parts of your life are
rewarding, and delectable,
Some parts of life you will detest,

Some of the fruit in the bowl is malleable,
Some of the fruit is spoiled, grim,
Some parts of your life will be
pleasant, delightful and others may be
Regrettable, sorrowful,

Some fruits are tedious,
Some are compendious,
Sometimes dreams in life
will take what seems like forever to
emerge, come true, manifest,
Sometimes wants, desires in life
materialize and manifest right away,

The bowl of fruit is not a bowl of fruit
Without all the fruit allocated in its place
inside of the tureen.
There are many situations, predicaments,

that affect our life's' journey before we
arrive and reach our destiny,
Many a quandary may post,
However,
It takes every experience to shape
and form us into who are when we arrive to be,
Do you need a lot of endangerment,
negative experiences?
No!
But,
God will take each and every one of them
and make a beautiful outcome regardless of
who is agreeable or objectionable
to what He will form as a wonderful,
copacetic, sustainable outcome,

Each piece of fruit represents a gratifying or
complicated experience,
You need all of the fruit to have a bowl of
edible, appealing fruit to consume,

You also need experiences in life pleasant
And some uncomfortable causing friction to
to hopefully bring you to evolving into a mature,
radiant, beaming adult,
That is masterful, vigorous, able-bodied, righteous,
secure, intelligent evolved human being.

Exaggeration

Penny
Penny was so thirsty until she drank a river
Of Kool aid drink while waiting for my return.
There was little or none left for me. She said that
she was thirsty and bored like a hermit crab inside his
shell waiting for me to catch up and reappear. After
rushing to meet up with her,
I was as tired as an ant who carried food or
materials on
his back to the sand cave. But we were as excited as
popping balloons once we met up with each other
during
the race. Now, we are as happy as waving banners on
on display waiting for their champions since finally the
race

is almost over. Some doughnuts are smaller
than quarters and some appear to be wider than a
small
swimming pool. I am as scared as the sun hiding
behind
the clouds to eat to many of them but Penny may be
angrier than a bug in a web if I do not eat one or more
when
eating the donuts with her consumed. So I will eat one
or two so
that we together will be as happy as two runway
models having a
great show once the race is all over and now fasting and
starving to look splendid for a moment is not what we
will choose.

Ironic Similes

The window was as clear as illuminating sun sparkles
gleaming off
Of waves.
His skin is as soft as sand paper.
She is as nice as a bull in the ring.

He is as fast as a caterpillar.
It was as stuck as crazy glue stuck on an object.
She was as quiet as glass breaking.
His outfit is as bright as first fallen, glistening snow.
She is as angry as blooming flower.

VASE

We did not break the vases, not mom's, oh no,
So when going pass them, go very slow, slow,
Sometimes pass them we would run,
But no one dared to go pass any vase, no not one,
No one wanted to feel a sense of dooming woe,
We stubbed many a finger, we stubbed many a toe,
But never break any vase or your favor with mom
is low,
It would not matter if you were her daughter or son,
Not mom's, oh no,

Always make sure her vases to for sure to shun,
And then you will be allowed to play out in the sun,
Mom's good graces I always wanted upon me
bestowed,
If you want your face a glow, pockets with dough,
Then in the house you must try not to run,
Daughter or son,
We did not break the vases, not mom's, oh no,
No, none!

Senryu

WORSE
Sometimes it gets worse,
When you need just better, now,
Keep praying, Keep faith.

BETTER

No one knows better,
Judging is what most offer,
God offers His help.

AIRY

Can you walk airy,
Seemingly without support,
Vague, quiet, needing God.

ANSWER

Where is the answer,
How long do I keep praying,
Is the answer soon?

SURE

You must be quite sure,
If rejected, stay secure,
Fade not in shadows.

SEDOKA

REMEMBER
Remember to think,
Sometimes chaos stops your thoughts,
Remember, calm down, just rest.

SUNSETS

Sunsets remind you,
Sunsets remind you of God,
You are awed at the glory.

FAMILY

Family is there,
You are in God's family,
God counts you in here.

PAIN

No one escapes it,
It will toss you all about,
Many kinds of pain.

I LOVE THAT

THE DRESS
I love that dress,
Its' just the best,
Like a spoonful or two of
honey that tea loves to twirl with,
I said I love that dress,
Like a girl loves to decorate
her world with flowers,
I really love the dress,
Love to lay the dress out and
admire all the details,
Trimmings, and sparkling things,
Lace with ruffles and a dab of
sparkle makes it ever so special,
Especially in the morning,
I love to pull it out,

It is always among the many
choices of what I ponder to
wear,
In the evenings when I go out,
I love to twirl around in it,
Love to try different accessories
that coordinate and compliment,
I also like styling my hair and
And,
This dress is just right for any
evening event or affair,
I love that dress because it reminds
me of pleasant things and brings much
joy to me.
I really adore that dress!

LESSONS

OPINIONS

I'm learning that the only
opinion that matters is the
one that God has of you,
And, I'm learning that once
you understand right from
wrong and try your best
to be friendly and get along,
If folks do not care for,
Acknowledge you,
It doesn't and will not matter,
God will open doors, bless and
Grant you favor and provide
abundantly for you,
And I am learning to finally
love myself,
To find those with a kindred
spirit,
To not let the noise of the
crowd distract my progress,
To do what is best without
regret,
It has taken an awful long time,
But,
I'm learning,
Not to be a person who
takes on somebody else's identity,
But to celebrating me,
To be secure, radiant and free,
When I am in the midst of a crowd,
I am just as proud and confident of
all the wonderful attributes that are
from me glowing,
And I'm learning to accept that I am
not perfect but also without excuse,
And I am learning that I, as a human being,
am helpful, beautiful, expressive and unique,
And I am learning although sometimes it really
hurts me that I will make mistakes, and that
some one's heart a time or two I will break,
Not to sit and join in with anyone who simply
tries to put me down,
Tolerate my presence,
Kill my very being because
they have hatred seething,
Who wants me with a very low
opinion of myself,
and then feel rejected and confused
when others are around,
And I am learning that I am not to
Take myself or life to seriously and
that to relax and not let bondages,
chains, low self-esteem, anything
negative dwell near me,
No system, no person,
No circumstance, and nothing
ahead or in advance,
I'm learning,
When I finally got myself together,
When I took on God's view,
When I did not compare myself with you,
When I prayed, and prayed,
And cried over and over and over,
More than a time or two,
I learned not to pay attention to you,
I'm learning that it does take much
To overcome and to make it through,
Much to understand that you will always
be evolving into a spectacular human
no matter where you live or be,
I am learning that it is simply much
easier to simply be me.

COLOR

BLUE
The color is blue,
Oceans and skies are blue,
Also blueberries too,
Water and juice sound like
blue,
Blue fish swimming in the blue
ocean too,
There are blueberries, blue poppy seeds,
And blue cheeses are things that are edible
Blue,

Flowers, like blue bells, a sapphire gem,
And blue feathers feel like blue,
The blue Jay,
Dragon flies,
The blue butterfly,
For-get-me-not flowers,
The planet Uranus,
Are all blue too,
Isn't it amazing all the things
that are naturally blue.

5W

Common Sense
Who removed common sense
from folks heads?
What was the response when
folks noted it dead?
Where is the place where it can

again be found and brought back
to life?
Why hasn't there been a mass
movement to recall it day and
Night?

Rhyme

RHYME ACTION
Once upon a time,
I caught a little rhyme,
I set it in a boat,
But it turned into a goat,
I chased it down by the lake,
But it sat at a table and began
to eat cake,
I scooped it on top of cream,
But it looked at me very mean,
I caught it in a dream,

But it tickled my stomach and
Feet,
I followed it by the fence,
But a flower growing it began to
Pretend,
When I washed it,
It became a beautiful sturdy
piece of fabric,
Then it turned into a kite and
Flew far out of sight!

NATURE PERSONIFIED

The Rain
The rain falls down,
It disperses from the
clouds that have discharged them,
It washes the atmosphere,
The earth,
The air and all of natures' creations
like the birds, trees, mountains,
Roof tops, cars and even the
ground, the roads and streets,
It feeds the flowers, trees, plants,
And all living things,
It fills the oceans with more water,
Ponds, rivers, lakes and seas,
If you are out in it, you will get a rain
Shower bath and so it may even wash

you and me,
Rain is cumulated in the clouds until
dispersed,
And when the clouds turn grey,
You can expect snow, hail, or sleet,
And definitely more rain to fall down
from the clouds to earth,
So take shelter when it is pouring
torrential waves,
Be sure to find your boots and
Rain gear if in it you must be or stay,
If the rain is misty or soft falling,
Out in you may jump up and down,
Splash in puddles,
Simply rain play.

SONNET
THE HUMANITARIAN

The proclamation and affirmation,
States that of a humanitarian,
A derived concept in evolution,
Most voiced by an authoritarian,

Character of kindness, benevolence,
Awareness of the deprived, suffering,
Through their life are missions, and evidence,
Responding from innate care, observing's,

They'll alleviate dire circumstances,
They find solutions, simple and present,
They expand successfully through distance,
Ameliorating hurt that would worsen,

Humanitarians are people of faith,
Humanitarians act, not debate,

They are like chameleons, making all good,
You will not find them all day in office,
They are interactive in neighborhoods,
They live in villages, towns, all places,

They are not of a certain culture or age,
They aren't necessarily educated,
They do not need to have, take center stage,
They're intuitive, They regenerate,

Individuals are viewed with value,
All humans to them are significant,
Their influence in the world, veers,
 doubles,
They're dedicated to task, diligent,

Humanitarians transpose life's woes,
Metamorphosing meager to ease flow,

They are the Florence Nightingale's in life,
Alleviating suffering right now,
Abolishing torture, slavery, fright,
Not moved, alarmed by the faces of frowns,

Marquis de Condorcet, 1789.
Declared Declaration Of Rights of Man,
Erasmus wrote state of felons plights, time,
Martin L. King, vied civil rights stand,

Today, Connie Siskowski, demonstrates,
Noting young taking care of ill love ones,
Providing books for those in need B. Kate,
And all who raise the young until full grown,

Humanitarians aren't always noticed,
Most go unknown, even unloved, or noted.

THE FLORAL EXPRESSIONS

They are,
Treasured, splendid beauties,
Fragrant and alluring, intricate
and many are rare,
And,
I surely admire the beauty of what
God creatively, ingeniously placed here,
Flowers,
Perennials,
Florets,
Flourishing efflorescence's,
Created by an awesome God,
Who positioned them throughout His
terrestrial sphere,
Us mortals gave them emotional
significance, and their beauty is undaunted
No matter the floret,
And that does too include the greenery,
Nonpareil in splendor,
For no matter what the expression of care,
Flower language is what is in expression here,
Aster is for love, daintiness, patience,
Nothing more delightful than a dainty female
who is awaiting her prince charming,

To shower her with passionate love,
Romance, divine union and tender care,
Tulips are for declaring your love,
To someone you so admire,
And they in turn are overjoyed from this
bouquet of expression from you,
Red Roses are for love and desire,
A platonic, pure expression, and not lust,
But,
Decent, transcendent, concrete, substantial,
Mature expressions and committed feelings
subdued,
Red carnations are for love and admiration,
Mostly seen worn in festive celebrations,
Zinnias are for lasting affections,
Seems like they would be a popular selection,
Yet, unless you understand flower language,
They are simply adored mostly and placed on
display,
Wherever they are arrayed,
And many are however arranged beautifully
in a vase,
The Red Rose is the most popular because most
all know and consider it to express genuine love,

And the Lilly is related mainly with Christ who
gave to mankind the purest of love,
The love of God our Heavenly Father,
Then there are Anemones that stand for
unfading love,
We should plant a lot more of these across
the lands and seas,
Where ever flowers bloom,
Because they are especially in dire need,
The White Lilly is for modesty and virginity,
The White Lilacs is for innocence and humility,
The Purple Lilac is for first love,
The Peony means healing, happy marriage, and
happy life,
The White carnation is for innocence and pure love,
The Azalea is for fragile passion and womanhood,
Being presented from your prince charming on
the honeymoon seems perfect, Godly, just right,
Daffodil is for regard and chivalry, so place them
in the house to represent your man, husbands
protection of you as God ordained and planned,
Anthodium is for hospitality,
Happiness and abundance,

Chrysanthemum is for fidelity, and optimism,
"You are a wonderful friend,"
What a pleasant way to show appreciation,
Adoration,
The Daisy is for loyal love and I'll never tell,
The Gladiolus is for strength of character,
Also,
"I'm sincere,"
The Yarrow is for healing,
The Gerbera is for cheerfulness,
The Marjoram is for comfort and consolation,
Sweet Basil is for good luck,
The Dark pink rose is for thank you,
Light pink is for admiration,
No matter the occasion or emotional expression,
There is a flower of representation,
There are ones that deal with gloom and rejection
feelings too,
I have presented here just a few of the ones with
positive meanings and expressions,
The expressions of wisdom behind all others I
purposely left up for seeking to you.

Today

Today,
My plans are to bring a smile,
To walk a mile in someone else's
blues,
To be the comfort that they seek,
To supply the strength and consolation
for a soul who may land a problem at my
feet,
Today I plan to be someone new,
I plan to fulfill and be the help
that may be hard to find,
To be the one who does and do,
The one who is there in just the
nick of time,
Today my plan is to be attentive,
To be respectful as much as possible,
To be entertaining,
Delightful and charming,
Today I plan to work hard and finish
my tasks,
To be genuine,
Innovational,
The very best,
Surely one of a kind,
I plan to be creative, precocious,
And not abandon my assignments,
Not procrastinate, or be tardy,
Intolerably, unprepared, or inefficient,
But studious, amazing, celebrated,
Today I will make relaxation time for my mind,
I will do much for others,
But today,
I will not fail to also do for myself,
I will pay close attention to my emotional and
physical health,
Today I will remember to count my blessings,
To look around me and acknowledge that
God has given me a plenty,
Today I will look for someone to console

and to bless abundantly,
I will share,
And not be stingy,
I will give to them freely and not
begrudgingly,
Just like God does with me,
I will demonstrate love, kindness, care,
Because for me,
God is always there,
Today I will pray for God to help me to be,
Everything that's obtainable within reason,
Throughout the day, and along the paths that
I encounter and with whomever comes my way,
Today I will,
Not make horrid demands,
Or have corrupt expectations,
That may bring about frustrations, bitterness,
And loss of communication,
Today I will be free from un-forgiveness,
Cruelty and maliciousness,
I will not be vile or wicked,
I will not elicit,
Jealousness and madness,
Strife or sorrow,
Grief or pain,
I will ask God today to make me a blessing,
And violence disdain,
If there are any problems or disappointments,
Aggravations or distresses prevailing in my
mind,
I will surrender them to Jesus, seek help
from where needed and not let them defeat
me by also staying in prayer all the time,
Today,
I will bring a smile,
Be the best that I can be,
Because today,
The smile begins with inner peace radiating from me.

TROCHEE
WINGS

How I love chicken and fries,
Crisp, golden, fried right,
Baked wings and bar-be-cue too,
As long as its good.

Zeugma 6

She wiped her eyes and her tears.

He parked the car and the brakes.
She boiled the water and the rice.

She ran the company and the people.

He heard the phone and the ringing.

She jumped for joy and the balloon.

Villanelle

Onslaught
Raging, was the onslaught,
This storming aggression,
Had not wisdom did sought,

Now broken souls, morals taught,
Transferred indiscretion,
Raging, was the onslaught,

Wisdom obscured, hard bought,
Events in succession,
Had not wisdom did sought,

Evil bombardment fought,
Prayer and intersession,
Raging, was the onslaught,

Though feeling much distraught,
Seeking God's protection,
Had not wisdom did sought,
Yesterday, lost, bethought,
Sometimes void expressions,
Raging, was the onslaught,
Had not wisdom did sought,

METONYMY

10
We need your smarts

The walkathon needs our feet

He is preparing BLT's for snack

The soul singers are there

That is an extensive wardrobe

The troupe will be marching

Her parents are coming

This is the church pick nick

She has many sources

She will be fixing six dishes

SYNECDOCHE

6
He makes a lot of dough

She receives much charity

She hangs with the upper crust crowd

He is one of the cool cats

He is wearing a lot of bling

That hairdo showed them whose stylish

He ruined the whole teams points

Mirrored World

A mirrored world is when
All was good,
Reputable,
Unspoiled,
Life was just fine,
Swell,
Not perfect,
But,
And with,
No unusual sorrow, calamity,
ruefulness or pure hell,
Then,
Suddenly a mirror change takes place,
An aberration is now apparent,
A mirrored world appears,
An enantiomer is now present
reflecting your life on stage,
And nothing is ever the same,
Some mirrored worlds are for the
good of things,
And they bring great futures,
And wonderful changes,
But,
When it is woeful with profound impacts,
Oh how you wish you could just turn the
Mirror around and return the yesterday,
Baby born/Baby Sids
Cute and cuddly,
Small and pure,
Bought all the clothes,
In the crib cooing and secure,
A glance later, gone, flew to
heaven,
Now,
Grief that is wrenching,
Never could in all the thought
Expect this as an ending,
Wanting yesterday back again,
Left without answers,
Bewildered within,
Left without answers,

Bewildered within,
God did you abandon me,
If only I could turn the mirror,
On the other side and bring what
was again,
I ask,
Was the cause of it neglect of mine or
my current or former sins,
These are the ponders sought out
until peace is given from God within,
And,
You still wish that forever would
not yet for this mortal have begun,
Like most atrocities under the sun,
Now normal again,
Child playing snatched
Out from in front of the house,
Running, jumping, playing,
You have a good view for sure,
Looking out the window,
Walking back and forth while opening
your door,
For clearly you can see,
Then suddenly, gone,
Far away, so long,
No place to be found,
Searched all the grounds,
And now you ask yourself,
Will you ever see this one again,
Was this because of me,
Or the dangers that persist and be,
I think you would like or need a mirror,
Just to turn this all around,
It is not your fault that the world
Is dangerous,
Even if they returned safely,
Much to your sorrow and unending
pain you will not find solace,
Ever again,
Unless spiritual healing commences,
Begins,

Child sent to school/bullied
First time off to school, nothing wrong
here,
Bought the clothes and the shoes,
Styled the hair,
Looking so adorable standing there,
Off they go,
Then before you know,
Crying, scared, pushed and hit,
Surrounded by attitudes of those
whose safety of others they do not care,
Will not permit,
Theirs minds are sick, cruel, wicked,
Bullied, exploited, intimidated, rejected,
You ask how come,
Why?
I know that they look nice, in style and
are very friendly,
They wouldn't hurt a soul,
They give their all, their heart,
They give until their hands are empty,
Their love is reaching and forgiving,
Kindness defines them much,
How could anyone them envy?
Or choose to reject and treat them so cruel,
Inhumane and bitterly harsh,
So,
You wish you had a mirror,
To change harsh rejection,
To undue cruel advancements that will
leave emotional pain, unknowable trauma,
Unthinkable fears and skewed misconceptions,
To give them what they possibly need,
Fortifying them with strength and
Courage,
To balance out their kindness and good
deeds,
To right the wrongs and turn them all
around,
To impact their world with positive,
Assimilations in new environments,
In the midst of new groups, crowds,
To show up at different moments,
involving them in a lot of things,

Where they will make a friend or two
And then on others they will not
choose so much to lean on and depend,
Just another chance to make life simply
fine again,
Teen well to do/commits suicide
Suburban life, want for little or
nothing,
Income fine and so exposure to
The finer things in life take place
most all the time,
Although have the best,
The finest and optimum,
Somehow they are still depressed,
Saying quiet good byes,
Wake up, time to rise,
Wrist split, head tilted,
They are gone, expired,
They are dead,
Now beside the bed,
A parent sits there crying,
They will never understand,
Or ever comprehend,
The thoughts that swarmed
Their loved one,
Now gone, far gone, gone away,
They wish they had a mirror,
Just to bring back that yesterday,
And perhaps have the solution to
make it all better,
And so together they comfort each other,
They leave it with God and pray,
One day to reunite with each other forever,
Loving mom dad kills,
Here she comes, dress flowing,
There He stands in awe as she comes
down the aisle,
Hearts are glowing as tears of joy
For some are flowing,
The cake, the food, the rings,
The decorations, the room,
The bride and the groom,
Five years later, the family has
grown,

Two adorable sons and a daughter too,
Then one day is never the same,
Dad loses his mind and kills mom,
Her parents just want a mirror,
How can we bring back our gem,
We gave our best to him,
How dare He wrong us so deeply,
And then loving her him for a while
pretend,
Did not she give her all and tried
nothing more than to please,
Whatever the disagreement was,
It still was not fair or right to end
with killing,
And now we grieve for our daughter,
Who to us was like no other,
Successful life/wrong influence downfall
Walking with the best, want for nothing,
Total success, Intelligent with influence,
Confident and it shows in all that you
are doing,
But then one day you are led astray,
A plunging fall from grace,
Your life is all over and your face a disgrace,
The consequences are dire and you now just
descend to the thoughts of permanent expire,
They just wish for a mirror,
So that decisions made can be erased,
Now a start all over again will depend,
The weight is just too heavy,
Sometimes when you get to high,
Evil creeps in,
A lowering will come,
Find the lesson in the midst,
Then reconstruct your life,
Beautiful young adults/now drug addicts
Going out and riding about,
Just having fun, partying and drugging,
But then one day you're hooked,
Now no car, but an alleyway is where
you live and stay,
Hooked on drugs, wondering the streets,
Looking for the next high,
And only a God miracle can change your

fate, plight,
And bring into fruition your true
destiny,
A real life,
Because,
They really need a mirror,
To turn things around, to make things right,
Beautiful marriage ended
No one can doubt this pair,
They were seen everywhere,
Holding hands and making plans,
Children just as they planned,
But then one day, the husband started
Being tempted and strayed,
He turned their marriage upside-down,
He became beguiled and so the marriage
disappeared, it simply went away,
They need a mirror to handle all in
his heart,
So that he understands commitment,
And that His vows are concrete before
God,
And so them he has no right to
forsake and depart,
No right to be unfaithful,
To be crude, a pimp, or thug,
To cause pain and horror,
To abandon physically, and emotionally,
To cause terror, and abandon God,
The vows are till death do part,
Not if I feel like you today I love,
Perfect health/dire sickness
Born with perfect organs,
Heart pumping very well,
Fingers, toes, and legs move
correctly, grew up fine and well,
But then on one visit to the doctor,
It revealed that,
All was not well, and the diagnoses
said plainly that it is acute and only
a miracle will let you here on earth
for many years now dwell,
I think the mirror is needed to change
What was said,

A miracle is now sought and may be it can
be bought,
Because unless they call on and know Jesus,
Unfortunately the fate will find them
where time will surely reveal,
For healing care is found in Jesus,
Not always instant but it is there,
Drunk driving/fatal fatalities
Just a little one or two to celebrate
the occasion, just one for the evening
to chase the day away,
Just stopping pass happy hour before
 I go my way,
Or,
After all it is the holiday so drink and
drink away,
 Here is to you and one for the road too,
Nice to see you all, I am going to
be on my way,
In the car I go just slightly dizzy so I say,
Then all of a sudden "Boom,"
I just skid into a car that had a family of
four, and now both parents and a sibling
are gone,
I think the mirror is needed to change the
circumstance,

To help be more thoughtful, responsible,
And just to have another chance,
To rethink where and how much to
consume,
And that If the intention was more and
more,
Then treat someone sober to be there
and make sure,
That all will still be safe although I am
having fun,
And that my life and face will not be
shown in the media for the onslaught
that I have done,
It seemed so simple to write these events down,
And yet they are very serious for
each and every one,
If only we would stop and bethink what
to do or say,
And say a prayer or two daily which helps
to guide the way,
Keep God in all you do,
In what you choose and how you play,
Then maybe a mirror to turn around
All, all around,
Will not be needed on any given day.

SESTINA
THE HUMAN SPIRIT

No matter the provocation, trial, humans will prevail,
Strategies are contrived daily, just conquer, and
transcend,
Battles are spiritual warfare, the mighty will subdue,
Negative influences are impacting, just surpass,
Prayer is a powerful weapon, so use it to conquer,
Nothing can bind you, you are your best answer,
influence,

Your foes will always devalue your worth, the wrong
influence,
Never listen or pay attention to their woes, prevail,
Rise beyond their limitations, subdue fears, go
conquer,
You get your self-worth from what God said, so
triumph, transcend,
A bully loves to bully, they seek the weak, just surpass,
Sometimes discouragement towers over you, you'll it
subdue,

If it's against God's word, it is not your answer, subdue,
The evil one will try to treat you harsh, jealous
influence,
Stay with Jesus always, just ignore friction, it surpass,
Soaring through difficulties will be natural, prevail,
The human spirit is a natural fighter, transcend,
Your will is strong to survive, adapt, make progress,
conquer,
Legitimate blessings God will confirm crush, conquer,
Endorsement of God's will is in God's word, so foes
subdue,
Cruel goons will use everything to surround you, just
transcend,

The pests use evil unity to prevail, false, vile influence,
Backstabbers are everywhere, cruel haters too, you'll
prevail,
Your human spirit is mighty in Jesus, you'll surpass,

Though it may seem like a desert dwelling, hardships
surpass,
As you traverse pass interferences, clobber, conquer,
God makes soldiers, not wimps, accelerate progress,
prevail,
The human spirit is tenacious, trounce, propel, subdue,
When soaring with victorious missions, create
influence,
While anchored in wisdom, love, patience, maintain
stance, transcend,

A mighty warrior is the human spirit, it will transcend,
It will cross terrains, oceans, skies, and even space, yes,
surpass,
No limits, barriers, humans, or evil spirits, cease
influence,
Your influence and destiny are sure, outdo, conquer,
The human spirit will accomplish dreams, set goals,
subdue,
Trust your inner thruster, human spirit, exceed,
prevail,
The human spirit prevails, overcomes, soars, leaps,
transcends,
It does and will subdue all foes, conquer and yes
surpass,
It's a fierce opponent, that leaves a notable influence.

Villanelle

THE CREW
Our life never the same,
Suddenly facing truth,
What a shame, who is blame,

This is not a shell game,
A choice made by pure fools,
Our life never the same,

This brought confusion, shame,
Have to fight onset blues,
What a shame, who is blame,

All are guilty, explain,
He is one, step up crew,
Our life never the same,

How dare you cause disdain,
The courts await the truth,
What a shame, who is the blame,

Travesty now aflame,
Our life never the same,
Suddenly facing truth,
What a shame, who is blame,

Haiku

Anniversary
Anniversary

Champaign, Roses, Money, Card,
A day to enjoy.

Birthday

A Happy Birthday,
Balloons, Party, Cards, Cake, friends,
A day to dance, Gleam.

BIO

Lovable
I wish I was lovable,
Like a warm slice of chocolate cake,
And I dream of being desired like
An expensive cup of tea,
I am quite intelligent, loving,
Giving, caring, devoted and kind,
I use to soar high with passion,
Achieving goals set in my mind,
But now I find myself being
hindered by obstacles intentionally
mounted always in the way,
I seem to however still believe in my
Self, my destiny, loving, kind people,

Jesus, and God, our Heavenly Father,
To help and to protect and rescue me
Daily as I travel along the way,
But I am really just trusting for
Peace, true friendship, real help,
Dedicated, loyal friends, and
Those who believe in me and my
Dreams and who will honor and
Support all my efforts,
And not require me to change
Myself to be accepted.
Receive help, and just to simply
Be a part of it all and fit in.

COLOR POEM

TAUPE
Taupe is such a wonderful color,
There are shades of taupe such as,
A sandy color, the egg shell color,
Or the rose color taupe,
Things that sound like taupe
Are sand sliding through your
Fingers,
Creamy oatmeal being stirred in
a bowl,
And seashells hitting the shore
Being placed there by ocean waves,
And taupe tree branches falling
From trees after a severe rain storm,
Food that is taupe includes such

Yummy things like oatmeal,
Taupe cauliflower and mushrooms,
OR,
Perhaps the taupe shell colored
eggs too,
Things that feel like taupe are
Taupe tree branches, taupe egg
Shells, and taupe roses,
Taupe can change your mood
From hectic to a calm and relaxed
feeling,
It can give a sense of warmth and
feeling of elegance,
Taupe is indeed,
A wonderful color to explore.

5W

ATE CAKE
Who sliced the cake?
What was the reason
for slicing it before dinner?
Where are the box and seal
that covered it?
When will one of you step

forward with a true confession
of consumption?
Why I am I still waiting to find
out who this was since you
know that sooner or later the
truth of the matter will be revealed.

UNDERSTAND

Pickles
I do no understand
Why people like,
Pickled food other than
Cucumbers,
Why they pickle onions,
Although I do think they
those too pickled are very good,
Why also the need to pickle
watermelon rind, and,
this by far to me will never be
understood,

But most of all,
I really ponder,
Why eggs are pickled,
Why pigs feet are pickled,
Why beets are pickled,
What I do understand most is
Why people love pickled cucumbers,
Why people love pickled herring,
And why pickling changes food to a
taste that folks love,
Even when it is pigs feet.

NATURE PERSONIFIED

Falling, Twirling Fall
Fall comes in with warm,
Cool breezes,
That later turn into chilly
winds and when this begins,
Fall then brings chilly rains,
And this transition causes the leaves
to commence to change from green
to red, orange, and yellow as they
begin to disseminate, fall and twirl from
the trees while forming colorful leaf ground
displays,

After all the fall leaves have fallen
off their trees and are now brown and
lye smashed on the ground,
 The first fallen snowflake flurries make their
appearance because the season has a
drastic seasonal change called winter,
The interval appearing, and unfolding now,
And this takes place where and once
The summer season has come to an end,
Once all the leaves begin to freeze and grass,
Everything then begins to turn brown.

Quinzaine

Juices
I love to drink pure juices,

Is it its fresh taste
Or just me?

TANKA

PHONE DROP
Saturday evening,
Dropped my phone on market floor,
Battery lost, gone,

I will miss my calls,
I had to get a new one,
Always buy a phone case.

Pensee

DEN
Den Room
TV, Couch, Desk,

Relaxing, Entertaining,
Follow stairs off from kitchen,
Cozy, tranquil, and quiet,

KENNINGS

My Daughter
Homemaker-Indoor
Furthermore-conquistador
Less-poor
Brochure-tailor

Headstrong-mentor
Constant-favor
Intelligent-Creator

Practicing-matador

Always-servitor
Decorates-corridors
Positive-ambassador
Chef-savior
My forevermore unlike
Any other daughter.

CIASSCISM FORM

I am entwined with a resplendent soul, form,
A pleasing, enticing chassis brings bliss, warmth,
Exaltation, standing ovation, I yield,

The sum of these mortal engagements is real,
My appeals are for the seeds planted in torso,
Shadows tango for embryo, now afterglow,

Quinzaine

APPLES
I love to eat ripe apples,

Is it its ripe taste
Or just me?

CORN BREAD

I love to eat baked hot bread,
Is it is hot taste
Or just me?

COLOR POEM
THE COLOR IS YELLOW

Yellow is our color that will
Take in this poem center stage,
Natural yellow things are the stars,
The sun, the moon, chickens, and ducks,
Some yellow sounds would be,
Chickens clucking,
Ducks quacking,
And yellow ripe apples and pears falling from
the trees,
And when it is time to eat a yellow treat,
Yummy things such as,
Yellow squash,
Yellow bananas,
And yellow lemons makes a cool tasty drink,
There are yellow pears,
Yellow apples, called golden,
Yellow peppers,
And the skin of grapefruit is yellow,
And best of all for most would be corn or
corn on the cob,
The texture of yellow would be,
Yellow flowers,
The skin of yellow fish,

And also yellow sponges,
The good thing about the color yellow is
yellow power,
The earth is lit up by the sun rays that give us energy,
The sun rays help grow the plants that we
consume, eat,
All this helps provide the nutrition to keep our bodies
Healthy, functioning,
The sun gives much needed light so that we can with
our eyes see,
It warms the earth, waters, oceans and the seas,
And then once it is dark,
The other powerful lights you will now behold
And view,
Are the stars and the moon which help light up
the darkness,
At different times there are full and half-moons,
And the stars give destination points to travelers
from around the world who know about these
guiders,
For more than the starlight given to see,
And on any given night you find them twinkling in
The dark, velvet sky looking as awesome as can be.

COLOR POEM

THE COLOR IS RED
Our wonder color is the color red,
And there are so many wonderful things
About this color that can be said,
Things naturally red are,
Red beaming lights,
Red laser lights,
A red ruby gem stone,
The planet Mars,
A lobster,
Red flowers,
Red fish,
The heart,
And,
Oxygenated blood,
Things that sound like the color red are,
Red fish swimming in water,
Red apples falling from the trees,
And a red heart beating,

There are so many sweet and delectable things
To eat that are red like,
Cherries, Strawberries,
Grapes, Apples,
Lobster, Tomatoes,
Red peppers, Red watermelon,
Red beans, Red beats,
Red meats, Red bananas,
Red plums,
And,
Red salmon,
Texture red things are,
Red flowers,
Red veggies,
Red fruits and sea foods,
The color red is very nutritional,
It can and will keep you wise, healthy, and robust,
It will see to the fact that you get to grow
pleasantly old.

LAMENT
COMPASSION

I am compassion,
I dress in kindheartedness,
I need a generous heart to express tenderness,
Humanity, empathy, consideration, humanness and
Charity,
I am related to mercy, benevolence, altruism, and

Alleviation,
I vacation in mercifulness,
My job is rendering fairness, mildness, support,
and always giving encouragement,
I desire compensation, relief, softheartedness.

COURAGE

I am courage,
I dress in dauntlessness,
I need a brave warrior to fight fearlessly
all ruthless enemies that are ushering in
violence, intimidation, cruelty and the like,

I am related to fearlessness, chivalry, heroism,
A soldier of tenacity, spunk, bravery and
determination,
I vacation in endurance,
My job is have audaciousness, toughness and grit.

Australian Sonnet

PEACE
Peace, tranquility, well, is it still much sought,
A truce was what novice used often and wise,
Seems like conciliation, hard to find, why,
And disharmony, not good, peace gone, hard fought,
Pacification has most with frustration,
Humiliation is rejected and scorned,
Yet, you are in bare skin, nude, when you are born,

Impoverished souls arrive in hades, caught,
When will unanimity for patience reign,
Peace, tranquility, imperturbation, needed,
Hades souls arriving daily, their plight, grieved,
Who cries now for placidity, balance, sense,
We fight where there is peace, we reject our God,
Peace, friendship, calm, levelheadedness, now odd.

ALFRED DORN SONNET

PLAIN
Plain, and forgettable was my reflection,
Unembellished my attire spoke clearly,
Would she likely find a prince at all, rubbish,
The mere sight of the mortal is rejection,
Why did this soul barely show presence, appear,
There must be more than innocence, and anguish,

Beckon the florals, twirls, curls, splashes, color genius,

Place her face in cheval, proceed, this you must,

Her plain face was fastened, then clownish actions,
Squirts of color went here and there, all through her hair,
The adorner obsessed the moment, tranced passion,
 Abruptly, pretty face session ceased nightmare,
In the cheval was a color creation,
Odd, yet beautiful, eyes spoke flare, hue passion,

WINTER

Here comes winter,
Here comes winter,
Freezing waters, icey, dark roads,
Here comes winter,
Here comes winter,
Frosty windows, runny noses,

Here comes winter,
Here comes winter,
Snuggly sweaters, frozen hoses,
Here comes winter,
Here comes winter,
Windy-Warm-Spring time- So long Cold-there it goes.

LAUGHTER

Are you able to remember joyous, healthy,
laughter moments and times,
We all have at least a few of them,
I'll share here some of mine,
I remember the joyous laughter from my father
during Christmas time as we opened our presents,
Our toys,
And,
Goodies that he worked so hard to provide for
all of us siblings,
And his darling wife,
And it was seven of us siblings at that time,
Dad assembled the bikes, toys, etc.
Dad and mom,
Precious moments, Precious times,

I remember the joyous laughter of my mother
as she watched us siblings play with brand new
tea sets bought for Christmas,
Then,
My mom and my dad scheduled tea times,
Filled with conversations,
Tea and treats,
Oh how they loved giving their all,
Letting us be imaginative,
Letting us simply shine,

I remember how when it snowed the second snow,
That my mom would gather up some from the yard,
She would carefully scoop some from the middle
section, thickness portion and make snow treats,
She would add Kool Aid flavoring,
And to us kids,
This was amazing,
A Snowy snowball treat that taste yummy, cool,
Creatively divine,
This filled our hearts with joy and laughter,
Only possible in the wintertime,

And I remember how we loved standing in the rain,
How my mom would put swim wear on us as the

Warm, Spring rains would caress our little forms,
We stood there in the rain shower jumping and
 playing,
Laughing and chanting little rhymes and sayings,
And for us,
This was the norm,

I remember how my mom would bake the most sky
high
cakes,
How we grabbed for the spoon and bowl,
The mixer sticks,
As we pursued every drop of mix wherever it landed,
Laughing at each other as we cleared the cake bowl,
No fighting,
Just searching for cake mixture with faces aglow,

I remember how we always had skates,
This was the toy to always keep,
The entire neighborhoods in this activity would
participate,
Starting from the top of hills and descending down
them while curving, twisting and bending to
an appointed place where skaters and bike riders
at that destination arrived,
Where all met,
Parents knew where all were,
How much joy and laughter,
This brought us and our neighbors,
Especially once you learned how to keep
a good pace on your bikes and skates,

I remember as we grew older and we moved from
our childhood house filled with so many memories,
Mostly joy and laughter,
A few sad moments in between,
We were overjoyed to move in our brand new home,
Surrounded by spacious yards, green, flowing
grass, and
an abundance of trees,
We laughed as we ran from the top of the house to

the bottom of this new dwelling,
We could find hardly anybody,
From one floor to the other so it seemed,
Say where they were,
Or call them for the telephone when it rang,
Brand new neighbors,
Furniture,
Curtains,
Fixings and things,
So many new rooms,
Enough for our family without crowding,
This is when there were eight of us siblings
In our family by then,
We all made brand new friends,
Experienced brand new wonderful moments and
things,

Even when I went to college it was a journey filled with
Joy, laughter, enduring moments, and this is where I
unknowingly would meet my husband,
My John,
He was the most exciting of all the college memories,
We had so much fun doing so many things,
It seemed unreal,
Like a fantasy, like a mere dream,

I remember our marriage and this was
such a wonderful memory for both families,
Who fought at the notion of such a union,
But cried and dined,
Was inspired and proud,
To see just how John and I together put our

wedding together simply elegantly and classy,
It happened to be the last most wonderful thing
on earth that three of our parents who are now
in heaven and no longer dwell here on earth
would see, witness and there be,

But my favorite memory is yet to come,
We have struggled for quite a bit now,
There have been much tears shed,
Disappointments,
Dred,
Serious trauma and unwelcomed drama,
In-between joyous things,

I want to remember how we two finally
get things together again,
How we stood the test of time and this Godly,
ordained union lasted,
And our vows before him although by fire
was tested,
Proved to be a great testimony,
An inspiration,
An outstanding sensation,
With the adoring favor of God,
And surrounded by real saints ushering
in encouragement,
Strength,
The word of God and Godly righteous,
anointed prayers,
Determining and settling for nothing but
the best from this till death only do us part
God ordained union.

LUNE
FROST

Frost accumulates
on windows,
In the winter time.

LUNE
KALEIDOSCOPES

Kaleidoscopes turn,
while twisting,
it's colors around.

SONNET
MY MIND

The scaffolds, are filled with memories, trenches, views, fade thoughts,
I drive overpass, avoiding confrontations, notes, aught,
The extension of the platform does not change, thoughts, wisdom,
The brain uses crossroads to navigate slant decisions,
Sometimes I pass over wrenching moments, grave, peril ventures,
The arches should be fortified enough to aid anger,
The mind conjoins, loops and stores experiences, emotions,
Vague is the decision when processing, wounds, commotion,

After all, the scaffolds are a fortified mixture,
My mind will align all information into fixture,
It takes those hurts and pains and sometimes, it erases them,
This helps my mind, thoughts, emotions cope, helps keep things pleasant,
They say you display the intelligent realms of your mind,
I strive for a higher intelligent mind view all times,
The mind, my psyche, apperception can be perplexing,
Nevertheless, my presumptions are geared towards relaxing.

LOUDER THAN MY BROTHER

Louder than an erupting volcano,
Louder than an earthquake,
Louder than thunder in a fierce
thunder storm shaking my curio,
Or a car crashing into another car at
high impact that awakes me,
Louder than a car horn stuck and that
will not stop sounding,
Or an explosion,
Louder than a space shuttle launch ascending,
Louder than a Boeing 747 airplane's engine
when taking off the launching pad so take caution,
Louder than a fire cracker,
Louder than a powerful wind storm,
Louder than an elephant as he stumps, and tramples
across the ground while running from the tracker,
Louder than pounding rain of course in liquid form,
Louder than an avalanche that left trees wrangled,
Louder than river falling waters at Niagara Falls,
That's how loud Trotter screamed as he was pulled from
between the thorny rose bushes that he crashed into
as he was being untangled.

I WISH REALITY

I wish I had a reality mirror that anyone could
look into for free,
And that it would talk to you and say the things
that are your good or misdeeds,
I wish that on it was a button that when pressed,
 Spoke, and listed all that you were doing right,
And that then there was also another button
revealing all of the mischief, and misdeeds you were
involved in both day and night,
I wish it to be so because people often hide from
reality and the truth reject, despise,
I wish that it was placed in a big square,
And that it was possible to access it on a computer
from near and far,
I wish that after facing and then being unable to escape
the truth and reality of all their deeds,
That they, people, faced the truth and be willing
to change and no longer hide behind power,
people, groups, mediums, and technology screens,
I wish that all would understand that there is such
a mirror,
It is called the bible,
It is found and read everywhere,
It speaks truth,
It tells you of your good and misdeeds and now you
are able to push a button and access it from a screen,
It also comes with a voice that speaks it to you as you
listen or listen and read,
The problem is that folks refuse to accept the truth of
their reality,
I wish I had a truthful wand to make folks face
truth and
change,
Face reality.

RHYME NAME RHYME

Alec gives me salad,
Allen makes me a cake with bourbon,
Burt is quirky,
Lilly is silly,
Chaz is jazzy,
Donnie is whiney,
Dianne is tiny,
Stacy is spacy,
Barry is scary,
Bobby is wobbly,

Timmy is wimpy,
Stevie is cheesy,
Patty is batty,
Shane is gamey,
Sidney is angry,
Zack is quaky,
Maggie is crabby,
Gussie is fussy,
And almost everyone makes me bubbly.
(Whew)!

Ice-Cream Combination Sensations

I am Terri Cunningham,
I manage a Sensational Ice-Cream
combination store,
There are flavors in my freezer that
you have never tried before,
Divine creations to delicious to resist,
Why not do yourself a favor and try the
Sensational flavors from my list,
Same arrangement means one flavor on
each half side and then of course,
The entwine is the mix of both blended,
So try,
There are:
Black Walnut & Black Cherry combined,
One with them entwined,
And the other with two arranged in choice
with occupying each a half side,
Brownie nut and Deep Chocolate,
Same arrangements, Same entwine,
Apple Pie & Coffee

Same arrangement, same entwine,
Bubble Gum & Cotton Candy
Same arrangement, Same entwine,
Butter Rum & Choco Lava
Same arrangement, Same entwine,
Chocolate Chip & Caramel Peanut Butter
Same arrangement, Same entwine,
Butter Pecan & Cappuccino Crunch,
Same arrangement, Same entwine,
Caramel Nut Cluster & Chocolate Almond
Same arrangement, Same entwine,
And my list goes on,
But you must visit my store to try at least
theses 8,
Do not hesitate,
And then also so many more,
I am Terri Cunningham,
I manage a Sensational Ice Cream Store,
Once you taste a flavor from my freezer,
You will surely ask for more!

Lantern Puppy

PUP
Barking,
Or Sleeping,
Time to play friend,
Dog

Limerick Lizard/Brisket

There was once a lizard named Brisket,
Who ate flies and crickets,
And small snails in secret,
But the flies didn't mind being treated so
unkind,
As long as it kept him happy and occupied.

Octo Poem Froggy

Jumpy, green pond frog,
Curling flies for summer eats,
In the pond sitting on Lillie pads,
When the cold winter winds blow and
the cold, winter rains begin,
Under the mud he is burrowed safely within,
Its' green rain coat helps keep moister in even
when the outdoor climates are freezing,
Like a bean chair its coat squeezes out and then in,
Nature Migrator,
Feasting at the pond buffet.

Here Comes SPRING

Here comes spring,
Here comes spring,
And now the daylight celebrates, illuminates
spring with a "vernal equinox"
Here comes spring,
Here comes spring,
Flowers such as dandelions, daffodils, lilies,
tulips, azaleas, lilacs, bloom,
Filling the earth with beauty and fragrance,
Chasing away the coldness blues,
Here comes spring,
Here comes spring,
Now appears all animals and insects in hibernation,

The rabbit, frog, dear, fox, bear, butterflies and
ladybugs make their grand and awesome presence
after winter's long, nestled somnolence,
Here comes spring,
Here comes spring,
Bringing back the birds like the Robin that for the
winter season does the survivor act of migrating,
Here comes spring,
Here comes spring,
Outdoor play, pick nicks, gatherings, sport activates,
begin to fill up those cozy, warm wonderful spring
days.
Whoosh-breezy-there it goes.

HERE COMES FALL

Here comes fall
Here comes fall,
The leaves are changing colors from
green to red, orange, yellow, and then finally
brown once they are trodden under foot
and are laying on the grass and ground,
Here comes fall,
Here comes fall,
The weather gets chilly,
Time for nice warm coats, jackets, or sweaters,
Yet some days still remain very warm,
Kitchens are filled with warm apple cider, baked
breads,
and firewood for nights of cozy sits by the warming
flickering fire,
Here comes fall,
Here comes fall,

The length of daylight will begin to shorten,
The sound of leaves are crunchy once hardened,
Here comes fall,
Here comes fall,
The fall months are September, October, and
November,
The turkey strut is in and the pumpkins line the
porches and fences,
Here comes fall,
Here comes fall,
In fall you will see rakes, falling leaves, haystacks,
apples, corns stalks, turkey, pumpkins, acorns, and
cornucopias,
And most of all it is now harvest time,
Here comes fall,
Here comes fall,
Chilly-rainy-there it goes.

HERE COMES SUMMER

Here comes summer,
Here comes summer,
Time for summer sport outdoor activities, like,
Volley ball, tennis, soccer, Frisbee, golf, surfing,
Flag ball, and beach ball,
Here comes summer,
Here comes summer,
Now it is finally time for summertime activities galore,
Camping, hiking, outdoor biking, pick nicks,
canoeing,
swimming, boating,
Climbing mountains and please do not slip or fall,
Here comes summer,
Here comes summer,
Summer treats appear to help cool you down from the
Summer heat,
Like snowballs, popsicles, slushes, freeze pops, frozen
cups,
Just simply all kinds of ice cream stuff,
Here come summer,
Here comes summer,

At different places there will begin to appear,
Lemonade stands, food stands, firecrackers, sparklers,
Air Balloons, kites, outdoor movies, outdoor bands,
Amusement Parks now reopen all across the land,
Here come summer,
Here comes summer,
The birds appear from everywhere,
The summer flowers bloom,
The butterflies exit cocoons,
The ants build ant hills,
Time to visit the zoo,
The fire flies light up the nights,
The mosquitos bite,
People vacationing and taking scheduled air
Flights,
Longer days and starry nights,
The lady bugs craw and the ocean waters fill up with
Glorious, tropical creatures large and small,
Here comes summer,
Here comes summer,
Whoosh-Shiver-now it's gone.

DREAM ASSASIANS

I dreamed a dream full of passion,
For the future,
As high as the heavens,
It will bless my life,
It is to bless my family,
It will bless the world,
It will bless my community,
God gave me my dream,
In fact, God gave me dreams,
Why does God do such things?
Why does He inspire such compassion?
Why does the dreams given to you evoke
Both positive and cruel reactions?
As long as you never plan to implement
Your God given passions,
You will not have to worry or concern
yourself with any cruel dreamer assassins,
The executor, executors,
These be there reactions,
Turmoil distractions,
Demonic partitions,
Schematic, brass objections,
Objected by most all and shunned,
Organized petitions,

Ridiculed and stripped,
Hated and traded,
Ignored and scorned,
Threatened and left abandoned,
Imprisoned and left in derision,
Cursed and situations continue to
grow worse,
Attempts on your very life,
Bitter accusers, abusers,
Molesters, arresters,
Cowards and bullies you they assail,
They stalk; injure, assault, jail,
Over you they try your entire efforts block,
Keep you,
Locked up and lock out,
Demolish, or your dream control,
Manipulate and you scold,
Say you are too young or too old,
They imagine their combined
Inhumane violence, plotted
Schemes as the outcome,
And that over you they will prevail,
But your dream, and dreams are
Spiritual missions,

Given from God and they will
Come to fruition,
This how God blesses yourself and
the masses,
Bringing your dream to pass for Him is
But a minor task,
It does not matter the enemies,
Mockers,
Contrived shockers,
Hacklers,
Wreckers,
Un-Godly defilers,
Blatant liars, and despisers,
Informers,
Scorners,
Defamers, shamers,
Traitors,
Haters,
Or any humiliations,
Demonstrators,

Defilers,
Disputers,
Rilers,
Stress or
Strife,
Attempts on your very life,
Prosecutors,
Persecutors,
Attackers,
Foes,
And woes,
Or any other factors,
All that matters is God,
It is God given and that means it
Ends with an Amen!
He gave and endorsed the vision,
It is not up for debate or a
Convoluted, voided fate, or
No completion of the vision,
And although you may face the fieriness of Hell,

Remember:

Ephesians 6:12
King James Version (KJV)
[12] For we wrestle not against flesh and blood, but
against principalities, against powers, against the
rulers of the darkness of this world, against spiritual
wickedness in high places.
This battle is not yours,
It is the Lords,
2 Chronicles 20:15
And he said, Hearken ye, all Judah, and ye
inhabitants of Jerusalem, and thou king Jehoshaphat,
Thus saith the LORD unto you, Be not afraid
nor dismayed by reason of this great multitude;
for the battle is not yours, but God's.
And although you may grow worry,
Become desponded,
Tired,
And confused,

Doubting here and there,
Filled with dismay and the blues,
Tearful and fearful, or fretful,
Illegally imprisoned and abused,
Do not worry,
God will deliver and rescue you,
Bring the vision to pass,
Despite the magnitude of
Afflictions, hindrances, difficulties,
trials, or the odds,
And,
Those who want you mocked
And disciplined,
Then till your very end,
Reward and exalt you too,
Make you that blessing,
That He from the very start intended!

Stream

The depth of a stream will determine/show
What type of animals do/can live in this type
Of stream,
A glistening stream with the sun rays pouring
Down its warmth upon it helps produce fish life
And plants green. The sparkling sun rays that
illuminate pictures sparkling,

Reflecting,
Gleaming diamonds it seems are what attracts so
Many admirers to its sparkling beauty as its waves
Move at its own pace while carrying with it plants
And nature growing things, the little fish will also
Be swimming/playing there while feasting on the
tiny living beings, When it is shallow the small fish
will be there and settle, If it is deep then the large
fish in it will travel.

BREAKFAST WITH MY
JOHN

Bacon or sausage fried to his delight,
Doesn't matter because it always taste just right,
Omelets filled with what He feels to be best,
Whatever is bought or sometimes left overs left,
In a container sealed almost as left over,
Are what may also be included as a bit of this or that,
Such food items like perhaps:
Peppers,
Cheeses,
Tomatoes,
Lunch meat,
Left over steak,
Onions,
He will use a combination of these or as many as 1
to 3,
The spices may very from salt and pepper to Italian
spice,

Italian spice makes eggs in an omelet taste different,
It makes them taste yummy, each tasty, airy spicy bite,
John's breakfast may also include yummies such as:
Bacon,
French fries or pancakes, or applesauce to say the least,
It feels so wonderful when looking at the plate,
Prepared for just me and he,
Placed in front of his and my sitting,
And do not forget yes toast please or bagel,
Also fruit and juices, Coffee or teas,
Or cocoa that is flavorful,
Or hot yummy Maple,
Usually a hot and cold drink substance to please,
So,
Nothing like breakfast with John, my sweetie,
The better times of sharing love and what it
Truly looks like and is supposed to be,

BLACK LIVES MATTER

Black is a color like brown, tan, violet, almond, or aqua,
The various shades of colors color our earth, space, and skin,
So why is it bothersome to others that "Black Lives Matter,"
The various shades of skin tones do not define a foe or friend,

"I must shout it off every mountain top " BLACK LIVES DO MATTER"

The conflict with colors, is deep within, the spectrum melds, blends,
Not set asunder, neither appears as a blunder, severed,
But subservient, they amalgamate, coadjute for fusion,
Colors make the world harmonize, synchronize, concord together,

"ALL LIVES MATTER" "THIS IS THE MATTER"
<"THE FATHERS< THE MOTHERS<THE SISTERS<THE BROTHERS<THE CHILDREN">
"No One Survives Without Each Other!"
< >
"The Powerful Force Of Each Other"
< I Protect You And You Protect Me And We Protect Each Other Symbol>
"I must shout it across every nations broadcast that "BLACK LIVES DO MATTER,"
Twenty-eight Black People (27 Men and 1 Female) Killed by Police Officials, Security
Guards, and Self-Appointed "Keepers of the peace. From 2012 to 2016 last count:

Date of Death	Name of Dead Family Member	Age	Place	Was "suspect" armed?	Comments
01/12/2012	Donald Johnson	21	New Orleans, LA	Probably	NOPD reported they shot Johnson after led them on a chase and fired on them. He was allegedly involved in a shooting that left 3 dead and 2 wounded.
01/12/2012	Duane Brown	26	East New York, Brooklyn, NY	Allegedly	Brown had called police for assistance in stopping a robbery and police shot him.
01/17/2012	Angelo Clark	31	Little Rock, AK	Allegedly	Killed by SWAT Unit serving drug-related search warrant.
01/24/2012	Steven Rodriguez	22	Monterrey Park, CA	Pipe bender	Man in hoodie allegedly broke windows at Carls Jr Fast Food and police were called. They tased him in the face and almost immediately shot him ten times when didn't surrender. [5]
01/26/2012	Christopher Kissane	26	Cypress Hills, Brooklyn, NY	Probably	An off-duty police lieutenant shot and killed Kissane who he thought was

Donald Johnson,
Duane Brown,
Angelo Clark,
Steven Rodriguez,
Christopher Kissane,

There're reasons, wrangles, emulations, mixed interpretations,
But yet there is always found a body lying on the ground,

It is getting difficult to explain the remains, actions,
It appears no fixed solutions rendered like jail, money, spurn around,

It must be announced from shore to shore that "BLACK LIVES DO MATTER,"

					involved in a carjacking.
01/29/2012	Atwain White	17	Bushwick, Brooklyn, NY	Cane	An off-duty detective alleged that White attempted to mug him near the subway station close to midnight. The detective shot him in chest. A 15-year old alleged accomplice was not charged.
02/01/2012	Stephon Watts	15	Calumet City, IL (Chicago suburb)	No	Watts was a child with Asperger's Syndrome. Police reported he lashed out with a kitchen knife. Mother said he had a small harmless pen knife. Police Dept had been called to this house many times before. Had experience in dealing with this emotionally disturbed child.
02/03/2012	Remarley Graham	18	Bronx, NY	No	Killed after Narcotics Task Force chased Graham into his home.
02/10/2012	Manuel Loggins Jr.	31	San Clemente, CA	No	Loggins was a former Marine Sargeant who followed a daily exercise and prayer routine with his two daughters, aged 9 and 14. His kids were waiting for him in his SUV when Orange County Police shot and killed him on the assumption that he was a threat to the girls.
02/13/2012	Johnnie Kamahi Warren	43	Dotham, AL	No	Warren died after he was shot with a taser twice for being intoxicated.[6]

Atwain White,
Stephon Watts,
Remarely Graham,
Manuel Loggins Jr.,
Johnnie Kamahi Warren,
I establish the fact that since Martin left, new tribulations,
Sadder expectations, violent youth mislead, complexations,

I make this proclamation for all the world to behold, see,
Somebody please explain, exhort, expound, in fact, enlighten,
The names listed here are few in number, for the pain, strife, grief,
Tell me isn't there more to this than the proclamations heightened,

This must be proclaimed the same as I'm Black and I'm Proud,"
That "BLACK LIVES MATTER" All day, All night, in every city,
In every nation, in every town,

Date of Death	Name of Dead Family Member	Age	Place	Was "suspect" armed?	Comments
02/26/2012	Trayvon Martin	17	Sanford, FL	No	Shot and killed by George Zimmerman, self-appointed community watch coordinator who thought Martin looked suspicious.
02/29/2012	Raymond Allen	34	Galveston, TX	No	Police, suspected this father of four was under influence of drugs, subjected him to multiple tasings and hog tied him. He died two days later. Wife is suing.
03/01/2012	Justin Sipp	20	New Orleans, LA	No	Off-duty police officer thought Sipp looked suspicious.
03/01/2012	Dante Price	25	Dayton, Ohio	No	Ranger Security Guards at Summit Square Apartments shot him 22 times as he attempted to keep an appointment to babysit his own kids.
03/01/2012	Melvin Lawhorn	26	Kershaw County, SC	No	Shot by County Sheriff when he tried to avoid a drug traffic stop.
03/03/2012	Bo Morrison	20	West Bend, WI	No	When police broke up a party where alcohol was being served to underage people, Morrison ran away and hid on

Trayvon Martin,

Raymond Allen,

Justin Sipp,

Dante Price,

Melvin Lawhorn,

Bo Morrison,

No doubt there is skewed injustice to bear, acquiesce, really,

Since when is injustice tolerated on any level,

Well, it starts when folks obliterate their own culture, truly,

When rape and torture, harrowing of the female is let, peril,

When drugs rule, guns, thugs, jails, prostitution reigns, rape, witchcraft, shame,

When mommies aren't no longer mommies, and daddies aren't your dad,

When souls for social media is for insane violent games,

When the life you behold is what you wish not to have, how sad,

We must get ourselves together, love, stop the violence on each other,

Then shout from every roof top, in every city, and in every town, in every country,

And in every nation,

Across the rivers, the oceans, and seas,

In the ears first of our own culture and then abroad as proud as can be,

Because it must first start with me,

That my life, your life, all lives matter,

Then and only then,

Stand up and say it loud,

That "Black Lives Matter"

My people matter,

All everywhere, in every nation city, street and town,

					neighbor's back porch. Homeowner, Adam Kind, shot him in chest. He was not charged because under the "Castle Doctrine" he had the right to defend his home against perceived threat.
03/05/2012	Nehemiah Dillard	29	Gainesville, FL	No	Behaving "strangely", possibly despondent over divorce. Tased twice and went into cardiac arrest.
03/05/2012	Nehemiah Dillard	29	Gainesville, FL	No	Behaving "strangely", possibly despondent over divorce. Tased twice and went into cardiac arrest.
03/07/2012	Wendell Allen	20	New Orleans, LA	No	Allen, a high school basketball star, was shirtless and wearing pajama bottoms when he was shot by a plainclothes narcotics officer. Four children were in the home at the time of the raid for marijuana.
03/07/2012	Michael Lembhard	22	Newburgh, NY	Allegedly	Police alleged Lembhard came at them (four) with a knife. Hundreds, including the town mayor, attended his funeral and protested the police use of excessive force.
03/10/2012	Marquez Smart	23	Wichita, KS	Allegedly	Allegedly refused police order to drop gun.(news story very sketchy. The funeral guest book on line is only indication Smart was Black)

Nehemiah Dillard,

Wendell Allen,

Michael Lembhard,

Marquez Smart,

Hear me, I speak as the drum sounding voice needed yet ignored,

You toss out your solutions as if they were poison, toxic,

Love your God, Love your sisters and brothers, help out, comfort,

Cease violence, vexation, cruelty, excuses, revenge, mature,

You have no reason for this behavior, no, not none,

Get up,

Rise above this each and every one,

Because all lives all God's,

Now love the Heavenly Father and Jesus His Son,

I have listed the names of a list undone,

It saddens me to still have more before the poem is done,

But change comes one me at a time,

That is the only miracle,

As I list the last names turn to God, to Jesus his son and ask for forgiveness

Of your mockery, sins, before this poem is over, done,

They are waiting to only love you,

To enable you to love all,

Because without their help, you may not be able to do this on your own.

Jersey Green,

Robert Dumas Jr,

Kendrec Lavelle Mc Dade,

Ervin Jefferson,

Sheron Jackson,

Tendai Nhekairo,

Rekia Boyd,

						knife. The mother said the officers were trigger happy, that her son only had a small pocket knife and he was emotionally disturbed.
03/27/2012	Tendai Nhekairo	18(?)	Atlanta, GA	Conflicting reports		Zimbabwean teenager attended Campbell High School. There were conflicting reports about whether his behavior was bizarre or a threat.
03/27/2012	Rekia Boyd(only woman)	22	Chicago, IL	No		Shot by off-duty cop. Innocent bystander.

03/12/2012	Jersey Green	37	Aurora, IL	No		Green died after police officers tasered him after he allegedly jumped on the hood of a squad car and moved toward an officer. He may have been in possession of crack cocaine.
03/21/2012	Robert Dumas Jr.	42	Maple Heights, Cleveland, OH	No		Killed during a car chase and crash with police. He had been speeding.
03/25/2012	Kendrec Lavelle McDade	19	Pasadena, CA	No		Police shot McDade, a Citrus College student, based on false accusation that he had stolen a laptop at gunpoint. Carrillo, the accuser, was charged with manslaughter because his false statement "led" to McDade's killing.
03/25/2012	Ervin Jefferson	18	Atlanta, GA	No		As he was trying to protect his sister, Jefferson was shot by two security guards who impersonated police officers
03/26/2012	Name withheld	16	San Leandro, CA	No		A sixteen year old died in custody in the Alameda County Juvenile Justice Center. Neither the cause of death or his name has yet been released.
03/27/2012	Sheron Jackson	21	Baltimore, MD	Allegedly		Officer killed Jackson after he allegedly threatened police and mother with a

And now the poem has ended,

The message is a proclamation,

Does the promulgation reach your heart,

Does it penetrate your thoughts,

Band together for right,

Not the wrong,

Maybe it is time to sing again freedom songs,

For no one is anyone's slave,

For labor or sexual,

Mentally or excusably,

Jesus and Martin fought against these damnations to the death,

They gave their very lives and souls for these matters,

These and other matters that matter,

Such as your rights,

Your freedom to live, love, serve God while being safe and unharmed,

Enjoying life without threat of violence, terror or alarm,

But most of all,

Dying unnecessarily,

Lying on neighborhood grounds with no help to be found,

Uneducated and unmotivated except to do drugs,

Except to cause harm,

Insane, inhumane acts of:

Molesting, raping, vandalizing, burglary, or,

just an outright thug,

Whether with power or none at all,

Just a fool on a mission to get attention for a moment, or for a
season,

So it does not matter anymore the color of skin because,

You see, the cry for unity now is for violence from every culture to do
together no matter,

To use electronics as a tool, and witchcraft as a friend,

No matter the age, race or skin,

Wake up people,

Wake up friends,

Does "Black Lives Matter"?

Does any life nowadays matter?

Ask yourself these questions,

And if you can exclude anyone as mattering friend,

Then just know your life too or your loved ones will face a
perilous end here and then, also at the very end,

Love,

Care,

Serve God,

Unitized for the good is the goal,

From generation to generation until our lives end,

This message will never, ever become outdated, useless or old.

REST

Rest is defined as the refreshing, quiet or repose of sleep,
It means a state of calmness,
To abide,
To just simply pause,
Forty winks,
A breather,
Cessation of all activity,
Rest,
Will bring tranquility,
And stability,
Interlude and quietude,
Hypnagogic,
Motionless and just the opposite of clamor,
And Business hour after hour,
More than often we fail to rest from our worries,
Hustles and strivings,
Working and studying,
We fail to rest our minds and our bodies,
To rest from preparing and scurrying,
To rest from building and participating,
To rest from sin and giving in,
From revenging and avenging,

To rest most of all our souls in Jesus Christ Our Lord,
Just rest in Jesus,
Just rest in Father God,
Just rest from being seen and let the Holy Spirit now take charge,
Rest from stress,
And all your fears,
Give all to Jesus,
The healer and provider,
He is ever present,
He is right there,
Rest on your bed,
In a chair,
In your house when no one is there,
Rest on a blanket outside on the grass,
Rest your mind by relaxing and doing what makes you happy,
Do something exciting, uplifting and not anything sad,
Rest in Jesus,
He will bring sweet rest that is always Holy and the best,
Jesus said,

Matthew 11:28-30 New International Version (NIV)
[28] "Come to me, all you who are weary and burdened, and I will give you rest. [29] Take my yoke upon you and learn from me, for I am gentle and humble in heart, and you will find rest for your souls. [30] For my yoke is easy and my burden is light."
Just Rest!"

MAYA

How do you know,
I ask you again,
How do you know about this news,
About this spiritual soul,
They say that she took her flight to the heavens,
A flight to the heavens,
Say that again,
Who?
Maya Angelo,
That is what is said,
Someone said that her works, her missions, her
everything
here was finished,
Finished I say again,
And so they said that then she just up and left,
Left all she matriculated here, all that she had ever
accomplished through out
the pages of history, and time,
For mankind to moan, groan,
Weep about and pray,
Why if you talk to some others you will find that
It is the marking of a grand celebration,
Now tell me just how celebrating someone who is now
dead a celebration someone did ask,

In fact,
Explain to me what you mean by this,
Is what was asked,
And said,
This celebration is for the soul of a poet,
Quite remarkable indeed,
Gone to meet Sweet Jesus,
Gone to rest her head with his,
For most all, the interpretation is simply called dead,
But for me instead,
I see her with those golden fingers still writing new
intelligent,
Angelic pieces for the angels to speak out loud above
the luminous
Clouds,
While walking down the golden streets as they pass
saints,
You know who saints are right,
Those are the folks who lives became inspirations
to the
dust people,
Us I say,
Us,
Why when she broke through those heavenly realms,

The cheers were so loud, and thunderous,
Why the celebration there sent water raindrops all the way down here,
It did rain, here I say,
For a couple of days,
You know it rained down here all the way around the world,
But in heaven,
She now has her words flowing,
Telling the glorious experiences there on forever non expiring paper,
As the saints of all times gather to hear what next angelic verses she may put
together with the angelic saintly intelligence that she will forever display,
Why even Sweet Jesus stops what
He is doing to listen to whatever she
might compose and say next,
We celebrate your lovely soul,
We honor and reverence the time and space that you filled with your
Voice, song, intelligence,
Spoken words, plays,
The embodiment of the woman you evolved to be and expressed
So vividly, boldly and with undeniable grace,
Fashioned always by the truth almost missed between the messages,

The messages of overcoming of ourselves in order to be crowned by grace,
The messages of unity and love between mankind no matter the races,
The messages of uplifting of the souls,
The acceptance of the struggles,
While shocking others and bursting the views of those who like
To live in their own created bubbles,
No one will ever brace the pages of history as a poet, play wright, talented
actress, activist, like you have, and did,
So I end this honorary solute to you in words by you best said,
I rise,
I rise,
Until I meet Sweet Jesus,
I rise I rise,
Until I embrace my heavenly, transformed being,
I rise I rise,
Until my home in heaven I walk valiantly,
Where I will forever write poetic messages,
With those golden fingers of mine,
Stored in a place called forever time,
I rise,
I rise,
I rise,
I rise!
Love Ya MAYA ANGELOU!

BLUE BEAUTY

In the inner soul lye the passions,
Like fine spun threads with rhythms,
Bitter, blue and cold sometimes this may be,
Yet delicate and beautiful even in the bluest mood,
As you could plainly see,
Who nourishes this delicate beauty?
Who or what causes this blue beauty to reflect this
So deep and captivating image, so very misty blue,
Crushing chaos maybe,
Or, the other plants with their absinthial comments
springing forth so shrewd,
Yet delicate and beautiful even in the bluest mood,
As you could plainly see,
Was it selfish hurling winds and storms?
Or boisterous, hard driven droughts not letting even a
shimmer
Of beauty to sprout,
"No! "You will not blossom!" shouted the harsh, bitter,
algid temperatures,
Freezing anything that dared to peek a petal, or leaf of
any type,
or form,
Blocking anything sprouting, anything peering out,
Yet delicate and beautiful even in the bluest mood,
As you could plainly see,
Nothing was allowed for admiration, or inspiration,
No, nothing, and it did not matter the reason at all,
The temperatures were fierce and cruel,
They were bandits, gluttons,
They angrily engulfed the lovely, delicate, fragile,
blue rose with passion,
Yet delicate and beautiful even in the bluest mood,
As you could plainly see,
The vinegary forces endeavored to keep its intelligence
and beauty trodden down,
Pushed under, so that no one would ever appreciate
what blue beauty the delicate, fragile flower could offer

the architypes,
Typical specimens of the world,
They only wanted her scolded, laddened with sullen,
wilted frowns,
But then one sparkling, radiant, glorious day, life was
no longer bleak,
Granted was the freedom that should have always have
been,
no longer would she be impearled,
Yet delicate and beautiful even in the bluest mood,
As you could plainly see,
A friend, one day, called golden sparkles came her way
with rays of dashing,
Valiant protection daring anyone to trespass this dark,
blue beauty, the ambrosial rose,
and he saturated it with his pure love for her
nourishment,
Then, all of the creepy crawlers vacated the
premises and found elsewhere to pester, dig and claw,
Or land upon her with heavy crashing, and crushing,
And with the help of some fresh dew, and a drop of
rain or two, it bloomed with pure love,
Patience and encouragement,
Yet delicate and beautiful even in the bluest mood,
As you could plainly see,
The delicate specimen of rare, beauty blue emerged,
"Blue Beauty,"
Rare and delicate,
Can't help but fasten my eyes toward you, and your
intelligence,
Spirit stirring, reaching beauty and charm,
With exemplar, soul reaching radiant splendor to
behold, admire,
view, relish, and appreciate,
You bring about a comforting calm,
Yet delicate and beautiful even in the bluest mood,
As you could plainly see.

I NEVER KNEW

I never knew this about you,
I never knew and I am sorry to find out too,
How could you be so senseless, so mean and cruel,
So brutal and shameless,
And unbelievable Jerk and fool,
And just so you know, I never thought that way about
you ever

until you,
Did what you did,
And do what you do,
I never knew this about you,
How shrewd.

GIGGLE POEM

Twinkle, Twinkle, Little Parr

Twinkle, Twinkle, little star,
No longer wanted to be up in the
Sky so very far,
So He slid down to earth on a rolling star,
And changed his name to Parr,
He learned how to play the guitar and became a rock star,
However,
He got bored and all he does now is hangout at the local bars.

GIGGLE

Mary Had A Little Cam

Mary had a little lamb that she traded in for a cam,
With the latest technology quirks,
To ensure that it would definitely work,
And everywhere that Mary went,
A pictures was what she took,
She took a picture of some yams,
She took a picture of some jam,
And she took a picture of some spam and ham,
But since she liked eating healthy she a prepared dish of lamb.

GIGGLE

Hey Diddle Pickle

Hey diddle, diddle,
Changed his name to Pickle,
This made the cat laugh and so he wiggled
And did a jiggle,
The little boy called him Mr. Dill Pickle,
And the cow thought the whole situation was fickle,
So he stopped playing his fiddle and ate some
Peanut brittle and began to laugh as he dribbled.

GIGGLE

Little Jack Horner The Transformer

Little Jack Horner came out of the corner,
He decided to get into the movies and
Become a transformer,
He pulled out his transformer weapons and gun to
apprehend the criminals on the run,
He enjoyed his role and worked until the day was done,
He said this was far better than working on the farm and
eating plums,
So then he promised to keep the earth safe and the
Sky,
And then he said" What A Good Boy Am I"

LULLABY POEM

Count The Sheep

Count the sheep,
Count the sheep,
Do not sneak down the stair steps,
If you do,
You'll feel blue,

For in your room you'll stay a week,
Fall asleep,
Fall asleep,
Just be sweet,
And count the sheep,
Do not creep, do not creep,
Then in the morning they'll be treats.

CINQUAIN

Terri,
Lovely, kind,
Loves to sing,
Helps people become elevated,

Teacher

Perfume

Wonderful, Fragrant,
Gives pleasant pungencies,
Loves flowing,
Helps people smell adorable,

Scent

Friend

Colleague, Buddy,
Provides friendship, intimacy,
Will give needed comfort,
Acquaintance

Money

Bucks, Funds,
Provides riches, bankroll,
Will help with finances,
Currency

Baby

Neonate, Tot,
Will become spoiled,
Brings much happiness, love

Youngster

Food

Substance, nutriment,
Will bring nourishment,
Does provide sustainment, preservation,

Vittles

Colors

Black

Looks like darkness,
Taste like burnt substance,
Smells like burning food,

Sounds like crackling ashes,
Feels like dark velvet.

Grey

Looks like thick smoke,
Taste like smoky vittles,
Smells like savory substances,

Sounds like falling ashes,
Feels like soft burnt dust.

Brown

Looks like wood,
Taste like peanuts,
Smells like fried chicken,

Sounds like food cooking crisp,
Feels like wet sand particles.

Blue

Looks like the sky,
Taste like blueberries,
Smells like blue cheese,

Sounds like blue water,
Feels like blue flowers.

Yellow

Looks like yellow peppers,
Taste like lemons,
Smells like pineapples,

Sounds like yellow crackly leaves,
Feels like soft yellow bananas.

White

Looks like the clouds,
Taste like cauliflower,
Smells like marshmallows,

Sounds like falling snow,
Feels like cotton.

Purple

Purple looks like eggplant,
Taste like purple peppers,
Smells like purple cabbage,

Feels like purple kohlrabi,
Sounds like purple falling grape vines.

Pink

Looks like pink shrimp,
Smells like pink berries,
Taste like pink watermelon,

Sounds like pink splashing grapefruit juice,
Feels like pink flowers,

RED

Looks like tomatoes,
Taste like red peppers,
Smells like red beats,

Sound like red apples falling,
Feels like red strawberries,

Green

Looks like green leaves,
Sounds like green splashing waves,
Feels like green broccoli,

Taste like green cucumbers,
Smells like green grass.

Couplets Cake

Here is the cake,
That was baked.

Onions

Here are the onions,
They do not cure bunions.

Lights

These are stage lights,
They all illuminate powerfully and bright.

Sun

Here is the sun,
When it is rising the day has begun.

World

Here is the world.
On the globe axis it twirls.

Marty

This is my brother and his name is Marty.
He dances cool, talks smooth, and laughs hardy.

WIND

This is the wind that blows,
And when it is boisterous, and strong it may make you very cold.

Feathers

Feathers are always soft and not hard like leather.
When placed in a pile, they look beautiful how clever.

Store

These are stores that sell goods for a price.
They have what you need and you can shop there day or night.

Noun/Adjective

WATER
Water,
Water,
Water,
Sea waters,
Lake waters,
Beautiful, flowing ocean waters,
I've only named these few,

Reservoir waters,

Beach waters,
You can see floating pebbles in pond waters,
You can fish and swim in river waters,
Flowing mountain water too,

Pure water,
Drinking water,
Don't forget bathing water,
Last of all, best of all,
Heavenly, everlasting water by God's Throne.

FLOWERS

Flowers,
Flowers,
Flowers,
Tulip flowers,
Lilly flowers,
Beautiful, fragrant, wondrous flowers,
Oh how they grow,

Petunia flowers,

Sunflowers,
Blooming, beautiful, red rose flowers,
Swaying in the wind daffodil flowers,
Flowers bloom most anywhere.
Poppy flowers,
Buttercup flowers,
And you can't forget the Morning Glory flower,
Last of all and best of all,
The flowers flowing in God's heavenly garden.

BUTTERFLIES

Butterflies,
Butterflies,
Butterflies,
Monarch butterfly,
Dainty Sulfur butterflies,
Fluttering, flying with gravity butterflies,
Delicately landing on flowers butterflies,

Anna blue butterflies,
Anise Swallowtail butterflies,

Graceful, delightful, Northern Cloudy Wing
butterflies,
Swaying in the wind Cloudless Sulphur butterflies,
Butterflies can be found most everywhere.

Northeastern California butterfly,
Montana Crescent butterfly,
And you can't forget the Leto Fritillary butterfly,
But most of all and best of all,
The floating, splendid, stunning, captivating,
The Angelic Wing Butterfly.

Lady Bug, Lady Bird,

Lady bug, Lady Bird,
Lady bug, Lady bird,
Lady bug, Lady bird,
Larch Lady Bird,
24 Spotted Lady Bird,
Crawling, nibbling red lady bugs,
Flying, creeping, rainbow lady birds,

Adonis Lady Bird,
Water Lady Bug,

Shuffling, inching Harliquin lady Bird,
Dawdling, lackadaisical, Eyed Lady bug,
Are fascinating, most not found everywhere,

Hieroglyphic Lady Bird,
Bryony Lady Bird,
And you can't forget the imperceptible Heather
lady bug,
But most of all and best of all the leisurely moving,
Convergent Lady Beetle.

I USE TO

I USE TO......BUT NOW
I use to go outside and play with mud when I was a
little girl.
But now I am a grown woman and I do not do that
anymore.
I use to cook with my mom.
But now she is in heaven and we do not cook together
anymore.

I use to ride bikes with my husband John.
But he is very tired after work and we do not ride bikes
together
Any more.
I use to have a lot of cookouts in my backyard.
But I am too tired after work and so I do not feel like
preparing food
dishes the way I use to any more.

Parts of Speech

Lady

The lady,
Gorgeous and towering,
Flirting and twirling,
With a man.

MAN

The man,
Handsome and brave,
Singing and dancing,
With the lady.

LION

The lion,
Courageous, Fearless,
Prowling, and growling,
To show his power.

5w

Tay ate them.
The ribs?
Last night.
At the party.
With his fingers.

5w

Claire went.
To the library.
A friend.
Yesterday.
On the bus.

5w

Ted.
Swimming.
The team.
Last week.
Motor boat.

5w

Molly
The choclate candy.
Her sister.
Yesterday.
Her fingers.

INSIDE OUT

My inside self and my outside self are as different as can be.
Inside me I am fearless, strong, unwavering, and I can do
all and be all that I aspire to be. I am overwhelmingly respected and accepted.
I have accomplished my goals: I will be on many stages presenting my
God given talents to the world in an excellent manner without regret, or
obstacles, despiteful dream killing assassins and haters. And, the only
ones there are rooting achievers who understand the journey oh so well because
it on many a day and occasion they had to cross these paths to get where they are too.
This indeed will be many.

My outside self is still shy, at times fearful, delicate but yet kind.
And In need of gentle, loving care,
Not taken advantage of and exploited.
Always looking for the best in life and people; Praying for answers and solutions;
Promoting resolutions and an end to all violence;
Waiting for the day to be safe, happy, cared about despite my imperfections
and seen as an asset always.

LIST

Woke up early,
Took bath,
Got dressed,
Cooked breakfast for husband John and my dad,
Took Dad breakfast,
Helped dad get ready for dialysis,
Left dad's breakfast in the truck,
Got home,
Cleaned house,
Got ready to go to the bank and grocery store,
Went to grocery store with Sister friend,
Picked up birthday cake and groceries,
Got dressed for my birthday party,
Went to party with sister Cynthia,
Fun loving folks came,
Restaurant packed with a few others celebrating too,
City View,
Band arrived, "Chandra And The Ryze Band",
Played like no tomorrow,
Danced myself like never before,
Guest too!

Sedoka

Freed

Freed from binding chains,
Relief from abode,
Pushing for brighter future,
Despite obstacles or foes.

New Job

Last one ending wrong,
Looking for mercy,
Grace found me and I'm aboard.
Hopefully lessons were taught.

Need God

God I need you, you,
Please answer my prayers,
Yet, you have never left me,
Your favor constantly sought,

Naani Water Dreams

No one exists
without water. It ran clear and free.
Feeding our fish and animals. The tribes
and future dreams.

Delusional Needs

Are my needs for my people's existence
delusional. A pipe to pollute our
lands and take away beings.

Little Shout

A prayer was sent up by little shout.
For the powers that be rampaged God's
plan. Our spirits, future. Caused much weeping.

LAND

What is land or water,
It's demand, need,
Except, when you, priceless,
No regard for our people,
Our existence.

LAI

DO NOT
Do not ask me please,
I fought with tears, me,
Those beings,
I pray for my life,

Despite all the strife,
My life,
Do not read in past,
I hope foes surpass,
Peace at last.

FREE VERSE

LET THE CHILDREN
Let the children write,
Share their thoughts with pen and paper,
Tell their inner desires,
Freeing their emotions and
Self-expressions with well taught words,
This is what is right,
Let the children sing,
Sing about love,
Sing about their God,
Sing because their hearts and minds are free,
Free from being an imprisoned being,
This is their right and what is right,

Let them sing,
Let the children draw, paint, create, and make things,
"Get out of their way!"
Do not hinder these things that be,
This is God's plan in the universe,
They'll grow up to become wise with understanding,
Then, and only then,
Will they rise to become kings and queens,
Do not chain their dreams, expectations,
Do not chain God's innocent beings,
Or,
Their God given dreams.

FREE VERSE

OCCUPYING
If you are going to occupy your time
and energy with and around me,

Then at least learn something that can
change your ignorance because not to do so
is retarded.

FREE VERSE

Enslavement
How can you walk through the history of time about
my people
But yet,
Try to enchain me,
Try to kill me?
Afflict my body and body parts,
Afflict my mind,
Assassinate my character,
Assassinate my dreams,
Human trafficking through witchcraft,
By phones, tablets, etc.
Openly, boldly with the help of my people,
The same, all over again,
My freedom,
My intelligence,
My right to celebrate and worship my God,
Who does you no harm but defends and protects me
relentlessly
since you have failed this deed,
My right to live with peace, and in peace,
Safely,
With safety,
And with dignity,

Not subject to rape, violence, illegal incarceration,
Kidnapping by witches and spiritual beings,
Given the okay by you,
Not even delivered or protected by those in uniform,
But also a part of the violence that be,
The force, a government that is supposed to protect me
and my marriage,
Not break it and form endless, godless unions in your
mind and others,
Not sanctioned by God, The Holy Father,
Jesus, the Holy King,
Well the enslavement by my very people as well does
not shock me,
This, enslavement, for our culture, is how it all begun,
Being traded to you by natives of the same color,
Living on the very same land, soil,
But,
Because there was love lost between sisters and
brothers,
We were sold to you by each other,
Not caring that the very life of all would be smothered,
As I walked through the museum,
I could not help but notice that there was no hall,

No room where blantly and plain for all to see the accomplishments
Of my people unending in every field like the black ABC's,
You see we start with letter A and list all black folk's names that have in
life wonderful accomplishments achieved,
That way you do not missed them,
They aren't overlooked,
Unmentioned, on the unmentionable list,
Left out of the "Dream"
You see, we need an edition to this vast grand museum,
We need to list all the doctors, Nurses, Lawyers, Inventors, Poets, etc.
And I do mean all,
From wall to wall,
And if not enough space,
Then build another for my sisters and brothers,
Maybe my vision is too broad but it is desperately needed,
How then will black children stop thinking that they are lucky if greatness
they achieve,
They will just keep fighting, murdering, raping and filling the jail institutions that be,
While more are built because they are told that they really are animals that need to be caged,

Not black, strong, intelligent, a wondrous soul designated for greatness,
A black beautiful King and Queen,
This for them will continue to appear to be a myth, a lie,
Told when needing comforting,
Stop killing your sisters and brothers,
Stop only learning how to shake your but and how to make it please,
You're worth precious gems,
You're priceless,
Your body does not belong to the pimps,
Your body belongs to the king,
King Jesus,
His name is Jesus, who long before all others died for your freedom,
Died so that you could be born free,
Stay free,
Live your life with grace and dignity,
Wake up from sleep please,
The evil one has sent an undectable spell that is controlling your will,
Your thoughts,
Your soul and very being,
Jesus,
Please help us,
Please set us free.

FREE VERSE

Born To Fly
I have always wondered why I have always felt an
Sense of spiritual awareness all around me,
Of my ancestors,
My God, my being,
There was always inspiration in the things that I chose
to do,
The things I witnessed,
The things I've seen,
Born to fly, Born to be free,
Always an inner sense to migrate to deeper pastures of
understanding,
I relish in the thought of that while I was very young,
That my awareness was enlightened by the King, King
Jesus my Savior,
Born to fly, Born to be free,
Not enchained by desirous fools, waiting to defy God,
Waiting to present their pitiful foul, flesh as being in
charge,
God rebuked them the same as their master Satan,
Mockery, sin, jealous cruelty reigns within them,
Dead, cold and sinful to the grave,
As the scripture surely explains and yet they think they
escape,
Escape God,
Escape God's commands,
Born to fly, Born to be free,
Never did I understand the logical path of thought for
Most other beings,
My momma told me that I listened to a drum beat that
Nobody else could hear,
The very rhythm of me, for me, from the king, King
Jesus,
She always said "Get out of her way",
"She knows what she is doing and what to do",

Unfortunately, your understanding of me will catch up
with you
some odd centuries later,
I have always been a century or two ahead of these
times,
Causing confusion in your minds,
And not mine,
Born to fly, Born to always be free,
I only break down because of the great visions that I
understand, and see,
And because you appear to be oblivious to such
wisdom ordinary to me,
And like an immature child I appear to you
while I wait for your awareness to understand,
Perceive,
Who I am,
Stop killing my being,
Stop killing my dreams,
Grasp my innocent, finite right to be here,
The right to fly,
Soar with destiny,
Born to fly, Born to be free,
Oh wisdom will escape me on many an occasion,
But the Heavenly Father will at those times cover me
with mercy,
As I wait for your understanding to become
enlightened,
As I endure the ignorance of those utilizing obstacles
to place
for me to suffer, for my soul to bear,
Born to fly, Born to be free,
But one day it will let me be,
Bring me resolutions,
Set my soul free,
Born to fly, Born to be free!

Oprah Poem

I am in a different place,
I am in an enormous space,
With delight I am here,
For you see,
This poem,
Is dwelling before" God the Father's" heart,
And with specials salutations as with "Mary",
The message of I love, See, Know and hear
You,
 Most of all,
 Is what He wants you to grasp,
To comprehend,
Know for surety,
Dearest Oprah,
Sometimes times when we pray to the Father,
Father God in heaven, we may not understand the
Schematic, strategical, mission or plans that
Father God has designed for our life,
And for the most of us and the best of us it is
through prayer and by faith,
Saturated with trust that we come to know and
understand,
Our place, our moment, God's plan, the spiritual
connection between God, earth, and man,
God's Son, The Lord Jesus Christ,
Your spiritual awareness,
Your grandmother was this inspiration,
Maternal grandmother, Hattie Mae (Presley) Lee,
We are all given a vision but we must want to
follow this as it is perceived,
We all are given a talent or talents and abilities that
by the
grace of God's help, and guidance lead us to our
destiny,
And with intelligence and awe inspiring wisdom,
You rose, Oprah, above every enemy tactic, all of his
onslaughts,
Ambushes, seducements, concealed blockades,
And barricades to be the phenomenal Oprah Winfrey,
God's anointed vessel doing a work that no one else
Could, ever would or ever will be able to accomplish,

No, nobody but you,
Your given mission,
And yet, I believe that it reaches far beyond what
We as a people behold, see and are fortunately
enough to
observe, experience because of your God ordained
province,
Yes Oprah,
You have made more than just a difference,
And now the matriculated accomplishments reaching
souls, and beings of every culture, tribe, all ages, and
races,
No matter the status in life and or positioning,
You and you alone with God's favor are able to reach
and influence,
Beyond most all's expectations,
Your life's work on display now while steadily
matriculating will be nothing less than
Dr. King's but from a different way of ministering
The message of love, unity, healing, giving,
while, intelligently, and purposefully living,
Being self-actualized while not forgetting about
God who grants the health and strength to do so in the
first place,
There were many an obstacle on many a day,
Hurdles that could have left you stranded,
An unfulfilled destiny, But you looked at the
fiendish enemy and declared that this was not
how things are going to end or ever be,
No, this will not become my destiny ever, no, not me,
It took this determination and awareness,
And, a faith in God to rise above it all,
Yet, you still are remembering to sing and pray to
Sweet Jesus because those sorrowful ordeals
that you unfortunately experienced were sent
Not from God's hand, but Satan's,
But God used them all never the less, the almighty
Father,
The Great I Am,
He orchestrated them to work in your favor while
carrying out

His masterful plan,
Your mission, the unfolding vision,
So,
Salutations again,
I love, hear, and see you,
Never stop singing to me,
Never stop praying, I am here for you,
No matter where you go, what you do, or what is planned,

And so with purpose after talking and communing with God
She goes about her way, knowing not to fear because she trust
His favor and relies on God's wisdom,
Like no other,
And what she is able to accomplish because of this
Is absolutely astounding, beyond words, terrific,
Just amazing,
Why:

As producer

- 1989 – *The Oprah Winfrey Show* (supervising producer – 8 episodes, 1989–2011)
- 1989 – *The Women of Brewster Place* (TV miniseries) (executive producer)
- 1992 – *Nine* (TV documentary) (executive producer)
- 1992 – *Overexposed* (TV movie) (executive producer)
- 1993 – *ABC Afterschool Specials* (TV series) (producer – 1 episode "Shades of a Single Protein") (producer)
- 1993 – *Michael Jackson Talks to... Oprah Live* (TV special) (executive producer)
- 1997 – *Before Women Had Wings* (TV movie) (producer)
- 1998 – *The Wedding* (TV miniseries) (executive producer)
- 1998 – *Beloved* (producer)
- 1998 – *David and Lisa* (TV movie) (executive producer)
- 1999 – *Tuesdays with Morrie* (TV movie) (executive producer)
- 2001 – *Amy & Isabelle* (TV movie) (executive producer, producer)
- 2002 – *Oprah After the Show* (TV series) (executive producer)
- 2005 – *Their Eyes Were Watching God* (TV movie) (executive producer)
- 2006 – *Legends Ball* (TV documentary) (executive producer)
- 2007 – *Oprah's Big Give* (TV series) (executive producer)
- 2007 – *The Oprah Winfrey Oscar Special* (TV movie) (executive producer)
- 2007 – *Building a Dream: The Oprah Winfrey Leadership Academy* (TV documentary) (executive producer)
- 2007 – *Oprah Winfrey Presents: Mitch Albom's For One More Day* (TV movie) (executive producer)
- 2007 – *The Great Debaters* (producer)
- 2009 – *The Dr. Oz Show* (TV series) (executive producer)
- 2009 – *Precious* (executive producer)
- 2009 – *Christmas at the White House: An Oprah Primetime Special* (TV special) (executive producer)
- 2010 – *The Oprah Winfrey Oscar Special* (TV movie) (executive producer)
- 2011 – *Your OWN Show* (TV series) (executive producer)
- 2011 – *Extraordinary Mom* (TV documentary) (executive producer)
- 2011 – *Serving Life* (TV documentary) (executive producer)
- 2014 – *The Hundred-Foot Journey* (producer)
- 2014 – *Selma* (producer)

- 2016–present – *Queen Sugar*[198] (co-creator and executive producer)
- 2016–present – *Greenleaf* (executive producer)
- 2017 – *The Immortal Life of Henrietta Lacks* (TV movie) (executive producer)
- *Untitled Richard Pryor Biopic* (executive producer)[199]

Filmography

As actress

Year	Title	Role	Notes
1985	*The Color Purple*	Sofia	Film debut Nominated – Academy Award for Best Actress in a Supporting Role Nominated – Golden Globe Award for Best Supporting Actress – Motion Picture Nominated – Los Angeles Film Critics Association Award for Best Supporting Actress
1986	*Native Son*	Mrs. Thomas	
1989	*The Women of Brewster Place*	Mattie Michael	Television miniseries
1990	*Brewster Place*	Mattie Michael	Television series
1992	*Lincoln*	Elizabeth Keckley	Voice role; television movie (ABC)
	There Are No Children Here	LaJoe Rivers	Television movie (ABC)
1997	*Ellen*	Therapist	"The Puppy Episode: Part 1" (#4.22) "The Puppy Episode: Part 2" (#4.22)
	Before Women Had Wings	Zora Willams	Also producer Television movie (ABC)
1998	*Beloved*	Sethe	Also producer Nominated – NAACP Image Award for Outstanding Actress in a Motion Picture

Year	Title	Role	Notes
1999	*Our Friend, Martin*	Coretta Scott King	Voice role; direct-to-video film
2006	*Charlotte's Web*	Gussy the Goose	Voice role
2007	*Bee Movie*	Judge Bumbleton	Voice role
2009	*The Princess and the Frog*	Eudora	Voice role
2013	*The Butler*	Gloria Gaines	African-American Film Critics Association Award for Best Supporting Actress Santa Barbara International Film Festival — Montecito Award Nominated – BAFTA Award for Best Actress in a Supporting Role Nominated – Black Reel Award for Best Supporting Actress Nominated – Broadcast Film Critics Association Award for Best Supporting Actress Nominated – Denver Film Critics Society Award for Best Supporting Actress Nominated – NAACP Image Award for Outstanding Supporting Actress in a Motion Picture Nominated – Phoenix Film Critics Society Award for Best Supporting Actress Nominated – Satellite Award for Best Supporting Actress – Motion Picture Nominated – Screen Actors Guild Award for Outstanding Performance by a Female Actor in a Supporting Role Nominated – Screen Actors Guild Award for Outstanding Performance by a Cast in a Motion Picture

Year	Title	Role	Notes
2014	*Selma*	Annie Lee Cooper	Also producer Women Film Critics Circle Award for Best Female Action Star Nominated – Academy Award for Best Picture Nominated – Independent Spirit Award for Best Film Nominated – NAACP Image Award for Outstanding Supporting Actress in a Motion Picture
2016	*Greenleaf*	Mavis McCready	Television series; also executive producer
2017	*The Immortal Life of Henrietta Lacks*[196]	Deborah Lacks	Television movie; also executive producer
2017	*The Star*	Deborah the Camel	Voice role; *in production*[197]
2018	*A Wrinkle in Time*	Mrs. Which	*Post-production*

As herself

Year	Title	Role	Notes
1986–2011	*The Oprah Winfrey Show*	Herself	Television talk show
1987	*Throw Momma from the Train*	Herself	
1990	*Gabriel's Fire*	Herself	Episode: "Tis the Season"
1992	*The Fresh Prince of Bel-Air*	Herself	Episode: "A Night at the Oprah"
1995	*All-American Girl*	Herself	Episode: "A Night at the Oprah"

Year	Title	Role	Notes
1999	*Home Improvement*	Herself	Episode: "Home Alone"
	The Hughleys	Herself	Episode: "Milsap Moves Up"
2005	*Desperate Housewives: Oprah Winfrey Is the New Neighbor*	Karen Stouffer / Herself	Segment shot for *The Oprah Winfrey Show* episode aired on February 3, 2005
2007	*Ocean's Thirteen*	Herself	
2008	*30 Rock*	Herself / Pam	Episode: "Believe in the Stars"
2010	*Sesame Street*	O	Voice role; "The Camouflage Challenge"
2011–2015	*Oprah's Master Class*	Herself	OWN reality show
2011–2014	*Oprah's Lifeclass*	Herself	OWN self-help show
2011–present	*Super Soul Sunday*	Herself	OWN spirituality show
2012–2015	*Oprah Prime*	Herself	OWN interview show
2012–present	*Oprah: Where Are They Now?*	Herself	OWN reality show

FROM:

From "Orpah" on her birth certificate after the biblical figure in the Book of Ruth,
To being called "OPRAH" because folks did not pronounce it correctly,
From being born by Vernita Lee maternal mom to being predominantly raised by
Maternal grandmother, Hattie Mae (Presley) Lee,
From wearing dresses made of potato sacks, to the best clothing and shoes on any rack,
From loosing a sister, brother, and her own child to gaining sisters and brothers
around the world and children too,
From poverty to renounced celebrity,
From misuse, molestation and abuse, belittled, and rejection, to love, acceptance, and forgiveness,
From wheeling, stealing, using, arguing, hanging out with the guys and telling lies to:

Winfrey became an honors student, was voted Most Popular Girl, and joined her high school speech team at East Nashville High School, placing second in the nation in dramatic interpretation.[45] She won an oratory contest, which secured her a full scholarship to Tennessee State University, a historically black institution, where she studied communication.

From as a child, she playing games interviewing her corncob doll and the crows on the fence of her family's property to In 1983, Winfrey relocated to Chicago to host WLS-TV's low-rated half-hour morning talk show, *AM Chicago,*

From The Oprah Winfrey Show, to *OWN: Oprah Winfrey Network,*

From no friends hardly to the best of friends everywhere and best BFF ever Gale King,

From executive producer, actress, publisher, author of 5 books and counting,

To being just the best,

From misdates and wrong mates to no dates at all to finding the man, sweet heart

Of her life time Mr. Steadman divine,

And now marriage and God on her mind,

We thank you Lord God Almighty for this blessed being that was created

and kept somehow I know by you and spiritual angelic beings,

May she continue to be all that you would have her to be,

May she thrive, be blessed and inspire all human kind,

How to: Live, love, overcome,

And not just die because of obstacles that mount up to be more than just a few,

Although they may be devastating and unbelievably difficult,

They may be hindering and overwhelming,

But they are never unable to go by or go through,

No, matter the difficulty Jesus because we all always have you.

Love ya Oprah!

God's Blessings!

1. Understand the next right move
2. Seize your opportunity
3. Everyone makes mistakes
4. Work on yourself
5. Run the race as hard as you can
6. Believe
7. We are all seeking the same thing
8. Find your purpose
9. Stay grounded
10. Relax, it's going to be okay

WHOOPI

When I thought about the sentiments
for this poem,
The word adorable rang loud and clear,
For you see this personality will make you
throw away your frown,
Turn tears and fears into joy,
Keep you fascinated with the entire story,
And if you do cry,
You will more than likely be shedding these
tears not in pain but in gleefulness while from
your eye sockets theses tears begin to pour,
Whoopi is laughter, giggles, sniggles,
And yes,
She is the caring solution for those sniffles,
She is the consoler needed when things are in disarray,
Those blues,
They will not stand a chance up against this lady,
They simply pack up and hasten, scram, disperse
out of the way,
She is comfort,
The best friend who knows where to go and find
Your smile again,
She is adorable,
But that is not all that she is because although she is
gifted with how to cheer God's world of people
whether
Near or far,
She is intelligence,
Whoopi is not European beauty,
She is African Queen Beauty,
Just look at her,
But the most beautiful thing about her,
Is her heart,
And definitely by all rights a born star,
Whoopi did not come from dire straits
beginning,
She had a good upbringing,
She knew from a very young age that she was
destined to be on stage, and entertain the entire
world amazingly, the masses,
In the film "Sister Act" she made this comment,
This almost seems relevant to her,
Whoopi's line was,
"If all you can think about is this one particular
thing, then that is what you should be doing",
This sure helped me settle what I needed to do,
With my life and other choices too,
Now let's go back to where it all began:

Caryn Elaine Johnson was born in Manhattan, New York City on November 13, 1955, the daughter of Robert James Johnson, Jr. (March 4, 1930 – May 25, 1993), a clergyman, and Emma Johnson (née Harris; September 21, 1931 – August 29, 2010),[4] a nurse and teacher.[5][6] She was raised in the Chelsea-Elliot Houses.
She is an active philanthropist focused on human rights. Whoopi also has previously called herself a "Catholic Jewish girl" but holds a firm relationship with God.
Read more at http://www.beliefnet.com/celebrity-faith-database/g/whoopi-goldberg.aspx#MIXm1OiBSPzp 682z.99
Goldberg has described her mother as a "stern, strong, and wise woman" who raised her as a single mother[7] with her brother Clyde (c. 1949 – May 11, 2015), who died of a brain aneurysm.[8][9] She went to a local Catholic school, St Columba's when she was younger. Her more recent forebears migrated north from Faceville, Georgia, Palatka, Florida, and Virginia.[10] She dropped out of Washington Irving High School
The name Whoopi is not her birth name but used on stage,
She has stated that her stage forename ("Whoopi") was taken from a whoopee cushion; "If you get a little gassy, you've got to let it go. So people used to say to me, 'You're like a whoopee cushion.' And that's where the name came from."[14][15] The name Goldberg is her mother's maiden name, which she opted to use in the hope of being taken more seriously.

Being a comedian is not easy,
This is what Whoopi decided to be as one of her
public occupations:

Years active	1982–present
Subject(s)	African-American culture, American politics, race relations, racism, marriage, sex, everyday life, pop culture, current events
Genres	Observational comedy, black comedy, insult comedy, musical comedy, character comedy, satire
Medium	Stand-up, film, television, theatre, books

Her comedic gift brings lightheartedness,
Exhilaration, cheerfulness, cheeriness,
Whoopi is jubilation because she is good spirited,
And resides in good humor,
Whoopi is also an actress, writer, producer and an author,
This following list portrays some of her starring roles:

	Title	Role	Notes
1984	*Whoopi Goldberg*	Herself	Also writer
1996	*A Funny Thing Happened on the Way to the Forum*	Prologus; Pseudolus	
2001–2007	*Golden Dreams*	Califa	Voice role only
2002	*Thoroughly Modern Millie*		Producer
2003	*Ma Rainey's Black Bottom*	Ma Rainey	Also producer
2004	*Whoopi*	Herself	Also writer
2008	*Xanadu*	Calliope/Aphrodite	
2010	*Sister Act*	Mother Superior (West End)	Also produced show on Broadway

Acting Roles:

In 1992, she starred as a pretend nun in the comedy *Sister Act*. In television, Goldberg is known for her role as Guinan in *Star Trek: The Next Generation*:

Jumpin' Jack Flash (1986)

Burglar (1987),

Fatal Beauty (1987),

The Telephone (1988),

Bagdad Cafe (1990,)

The Long Walk Home (1990)

Soapdish (1991)

Sister Act 1992,

Goldberg starred in *Soapdish* (1991) and had a recurring role on *Star Trek: The Next Generation* as Guinan, which she would reprise in two *Star Trek* films.. Next, she starred in *Sarafina!*. During the next year, she hosted a late-night talk show titled *The Whoopi Goldberg Show* and starred in two more motion pictures: *Made in America* and *Sister Act 2: Back in the Habit*. From 1994 to 1995, Goldberg appeared in *Corrina, Corrina*, *The Lion King* (voice), *The Pagemaster* (voice), *Boys on the Side*, and *Moonlight and Valentino*. Goldberg guest starred on *Muppets Tonight* in 1996. She became the first African-American woman to host the Academy Awards show in 1994,[24] and the first woman to solo host. She hosted the awards show again in 1996, 1999, and 2002.

From 1998 to 2001, Goldberg took supporting roles in *How Stella Got Her Groove Back* with Angela Bassett, *Girl, Interrupted* with Winona Ryder, and Angelina Jolie, *Kingdom Come* and *Rat Race* with an all-star ensemble cast. She starred in the ABC-TV versions of *Cinderella*, *A Knight in Camelot*, and *Call Me Claus*. In 1998, she gained a new audience when she became the "Center Square" on *Hollywood Squares*.

She is an Academy Award Winner:

Caryn Elaine Johnson (born November 13, 1955),[3] known professionally as Whoopi Goldberg (/ˈhwʊpi/), is an American actress, comedian, author and television host. She has been nominated for 13 Emmy Awards for her work in television and is one of the few entertainers who have won an Emmy Award, a Grammy Award, an Oscar, and a Tony Award. She was the second black woman in the history of the Academy Awards to win an acting Oscar.

In the period drama film *The Color Purple* (1985), her breakthrough role was playing Celie, a mistreated black woman in the Deep South, for which she was nominated for the Academy Award for Best Actress. In the romantic fantasy film *Ghost* (1990), Goldberg played Oda Mae Brown, an eccentric psychic who helped a slain man (Patrick Swayze) save his lover (Demi Moore), for which she won the Academy Award for Best Supporting Actress.
the Academy Award for Best Supporting Actress in nearly 50 years, and the second black woman to win an Academy Award for acting (the first being Hattie McDaniel, for 1939's *Gone with the Wind*).
Goldberg was honored with a star on the Hollywood Walk of Fame.
Goldberg garnered awards from the NAACP Image Awards.

When I see her name on the screen,
It means all these diverse talents are what the viewers
are about to behold and see,
So if it is unspeakable joy, silage, and entertainment
you want and desire to bring to the masses that be,
Please consider more than just a mere glance at what
Whoopi has brought and brings,
She is impactful in life with her strong opinions and
beliefs,
Just check out her moderator role on the talk show
entitled "The View",
"And since 2007, she has been the moderator of the
daytime
television talk show *The View*."
How can I say any more about this adorable, intelligent,
Witty, charismatic, dazzling, magnetic personality,
By noting the fact that she is also a mother whom has
raised apparently just as talented and as successful

a maternal daughter,
So,
How do we end this poem,
Alliteration,
By stating that God has blessed this sole,
And although a snap with drugs happened,
This episode is in her past,
For Jesus would not let that be or there where
Whoopi would stay trapped in,
He is also the mediator for sins,
And in her prayers to Jesus is where she
found her deliverance from that ordeal and sweet peace,
For Jesus is still the one who is blessing, keeping,
And protecting,
Now, and in her past as well,
And Jesus forever does and will be.
Jesus loves Whoopi!

SPIRITUAL ENCOUNTERS

God's Holy Presence

You can be dwelling in God's,
Jesus holy presence unknowingly,
With God's angels all around,
But,
Because to you this hasn't been discerned,
perceived or yet revealed,
You may not be cognizant of it, witness and view
heavenly visitations normal in heaven
beyond the earthly clouds,
From a heavenly point of view,
Appearances on earth aren't new,
Your senses are yet to be enlightened,
Then,
Perception awakens,
And the now moment peers through,
Suddenly a voice speaks and says to you,
A direction not alarming,
A message, this He speaks,
Take off your shoes,
Just like what was said to Moses,
Where ever you may abide,
For He knows you know the scriptures,
And He knows that you will understand that with
you He
is dwelling and that with you He has chosen in your
presence and heart to reside,
There are many who pray and request his presence,
And Jesus rewarded them with His divine appearance,
A loving, sincere heart Jesus rewards every single time,

Jesus will come also to rescue you in the midst
of the testing,
And when you pass, Jesus grants the
abundance of heavens blessings,
Just the same as Abraham,
Who was granted nothing but the best,
The Hebrew boys were thrown in the fire,
Daniel was placed in the lion's den,
After being sorely and surely tested, tried,
God afterward granted his servants awesome provision,
Because,
Daniel, The Hebrew Boys, and many
others chose to follow and hold on to "Him",
Although they appeared to be abandoned,
This was simply a camouflaged lie,
The presence of God was also a burning bush
to Moses in the dessert, in the daylight, in the sun,
and yet,
Not singeing, cauterized or consumed,
This Moses left all to witness for himself and view,
God's presence showed up powerfully at the Red Sea,
As the Israelites were fleeing from Pharaoh,
The horrible, wicked king,
He led His children while departing the great,
enormous waters that be, called "The Red Sea",
Then God let the waters flow back naturally after
the entering of Pharaoh's vast and mighty army,
God's abilities manifesting for all to behold, see,
Pharaoh's army, was drowned, gone,

No longer ever to be seen,
They relied on numbers,
They relied on the false God's they served
and not God,
Their Eternal Master, Ruler and King,
Now behold God's presence is in your testing and
trials,
For yet a little while and then no longer will you
suffer the vexing wicked on parade ever so bold,
Just like Paul who pursued the prophets who had to
hide,
Jesus came down from heaven and knocked him off his
ride,
Jesus administered a holy remedy to Pauls' wicked
pride,
Jesus came down from His throne,
Spoke to Paul face to face with His voice,
Jesus crushed, silenced the situation,
Saul's name became Paul loving Christ our
Savior ever more,
Sometimes your cruelest enemies are set up for
an encounter,
A life changing moment with God,
Hopefully they will respond like Paul,
Your encounters with God should be quite
different when born again,
They hopefully will not catch you in sin,
Each encounter is different and you will learn
how to comprehend, realize, each moment,
You must understand and know when you are
in the presence of The Lord Jesus, our King,

The children of Israel were beckoned to come to
the mountain to witness and see,
Have an encounter with God almighty,
Suddenly they realized that God was real sure enough,
They knew then that they were not worthy or
prepared to stand before the presence
of God The Almighty,
The ever ruling Majestic King,
Sometimes God chooses to send His angels beaming
with His power and authority,
Granting deliverance from wicked tormentors
or special blessings that will surely be,
An Angel granted favor to Jacob and kept
him safe as he slept,
And then blessed him greatly before He left,
You see, God's word and will does not change,
Jesus, God's son who died for you and me,
Grants daily constant provision to all mankind,
Every human, all creatures, all beings,
Healing,
Miracles,
Deliverance,
The best of His presence and time, everything,
God, Jesus loves to grant visitations to His servants,
Those whom seek His presence from near, and afar,
So when you realize that you need a divine encounter
From Jesus, from God on High,
Humble yourself and seek him steadfastly,
He will reward you with His awesome, holy presence,
and blessings each and every single time.

EMPTY

You may think that you do not want to
reach empty,
The emptying of yourself,
Any old remnants of a once was you,
But that is exactly where God needs you to be,
That way He can fill you with all that you
now and will ever need,
A new spirit filled being,
Born again,
Holy Ghost filled,
Speaking a heavenly language,
Useful,
Beaming with the glory of Jesus our Savior and
Salvation king,
He cannot fill a vessel at all that's already
completely filled up with everything else,
With sin and reliance on self, worldly things,
And on all other things,
You must empty all out so that Jesus can
do the cleansing, and Holy Spirit filling,
This is the only way to heal hearts that
need mending,
Jesus, the Holy Spirit will,
Remove all sin, wickedness, all soul impurities,
All hurts, and fermenting wounds, sour attitudes,
So empty yourself on your knees at the cross,
Then rise up redeemed, Saved, Delivered, Blessed and
Set Free,
Carrying and proclaiming the blood stain banner,
Carrying the cross.

Jesus Love

Jesus loves you and so do I,
Just look up at his beautiful, vast,
Infinite, pulchritudinous blue sky,
He made the oceans and the seas,
The rivers, the ponds and the streams that be,
All birds that sing and fly too,
Any small creeping thing,
All the creatures in the oceans, waters, seas,
And any animal that you can adore, see
All plant life, in-fact any green growing thing,
All lands, mountains,
Celestial bodies, the clouds,
And the sun that illuminates brightly,
All the stars that be and the very moons you see,
The rain, hail, snow, dew, sleet,
He made you, all humans that also includes me,
He made your mom and dad,
The babies,
He made the air, the clouds,
And heavenly host,
Everyone and everything that is or was created
in this world out of His love,
What would there be without God.

The Again And Again Praise

Jesus, Heavenly Father,

Thank you for the again and again

Answers,

Blessings,

Deliverances,

I know that I need you still again and again,

However,

I know that the battle you have already won,

Jesus I know and before all declare you as my Savior

And God's son,

Yet,

Having said all that,

This does not mean that I will not have to come to you again and again,

You are aware of this and this is how you said for it to be,

Depending on you for all and everything,

I thank you for always making provision for all my needs and

for totally forgiving my sins, taking away penalties and understanding me,

I so dearly need your help,

Deliverance,

Care,

Love,

Acceptance,

Forgiveness,

And,

Protection,

Every kind of blessing that I am in advance thanking you for

and that I am always confessing again and again,

When my enemies try to make me ashamed that I need you again

and again,

Strengthen me Lord Jesus with your anointed caring favor,

When I fall weak from the battle at your alter sometimes in despair,

Please send the help that I prayed for and need from far and near,

You are the God who never sleeps or

Forgets anything ever except my sins,

So again and again here I am,

Pouring out my heart,

Anguish,

Despondency,

Frustration,

Dilemmas,

Predicaments,

Disappointments,

Stress and troubles,

And yes,

As usual,

I need you again and again,
Sometimes it is family troubles,
Sometimes it is marriage difficulties,
Sometimes my selfish unforgiving attitude,
Yet, forgiveness is what I'll need the most,
Sometimes it is financial crisis,
Sometimes it is flesh control issues that may be,
Gluttony,
Sexual,
Dishonesty,
Temper,
Neglect,
And yes, I need deliverance form these or that,
Most times it may be deliverance from cruel enemies
that are
quite shrewd,
They plan my demise constantly and down fall,
The strife and ending of my life,
They plot and schedule my humiliation and disgrace,

They put me on display the same way they did you on
many a day,
They strategize my dilemmas,
The set up the trials and trauma that bring tears to my
face,
But,
Again and again,
You send your deliverance,
You apply your mercy and grace,
You grant the favor and answers to my petitions,
All my trespasses and sins under your salvation plan
are totally forgiven,
And although I learn righteous lessons through the
trials and
the load I through humility bear,
Still,
Again and again I thank you for always blessing me,
sending deliverance and,
Again,
Always being there.

Communing With Jesus

On my knees as I prayed,
The Holy Spirit of Jesus came to me and said,
Take communion,
I stopped my praying and obeyed,
I followed what He requested because I
discerned,
I knew that this represents his pure
cleansing,
His acceptance of my voice,
His acceptance of my praise.

Jesus loves pure fellowship,
And when He wants to purify your worship,
Simply obey.
Our Father which art in heaven,
Hear me when I pray,
Jesus, you gave,
And Jesus you saved us,
In order to purify our request
through you,
Just as you have said.

Desert Demons

Snarling,
Swinging at you with their words,
They strike at you with their
plans of manipulation and destruction,
If you do not do this, or that,
They promise you a curse,
They put their self in God's place,
They try to bring tears to your face,
They manipulate with fear and disgrace,
Where are they when you are struggling?
Where are they when everything around
you is going wrong?
You emptied your purse to bless them,
You did not send them words that would curse,
Yet,
Just do not send them what they are asking for,
All of a sudden you are promised hardship,
unopened doors,
and the worse,
Simply courses galore,
You are called everything under
the sun and no longer a child of God,
I thank God that my blessings as well as
All of God's children are not determined by
By hypocrites or no one else and that

includes all,
There are many people who call on the Lord,
But not all serve him,
God is in charge and has blessings that He
generously grants to every created being,
If we were cursed according to what we all
actually deserved,
Jesus would have never died for everyone,
Or anyone,
Because,
Some man would have stopped his blood
from being shed to render salvation on the cross,
Redemption would have been lost,
Salvation just like God's blessings are not
depended upon manipulation, or man's demands,
It is based upon God's care and favor towards you,
Without Christ blood that was shed,
In God's presence we have no right,
No blood cleansed claim,
God's blessings are daily,
He attends to you with loving kindness,
forgiveness, understanding, and
in his blessings you are included and
not excluded,

Especially when you serve him.
Jacobs Blessing

I wonder do we as God's people
really want to be blessed?
Ask Jacob about God's blessings,
Jacob knew what was best,
Jacob came from a mess that
He created but not on his own,
His mom helped out the one he dethroned,
It was already to be regardless of any being,
It started about a birth right,
And so Jacob now needs a heavenly answer,
Heavenly peace,
Heavenly blessings,
Jacob needs deliverance!
And, God's favor,
Jacob wrestled all night.
With that angel Jacob did fight,
He needed his blessing before the Angel
took his flight,
Jacob reached, and then grabbed on to the
angelic being tight,
To hinder his flight that night,
"Let Me Go,"
"Let Me Go,"
"Said the Angel,"
"I have watched over you through the night"
"Not so,"
"Not so," said Jacob,

"I must be gone for it is now dawn"
Said the angel,
"I will continue to grip strong,"
Were the proclamations of Jacob,
"I will hold on" and not let go"
"Not until you bless me,"
"Not until you make my existence worth
living, existing, and worth this plight,"
Not without the blessing,"
Said Jacob as the morning dawns light was
peering through the ending of the night,
"Time is near and I must take my flight,"
"Not until you change my plight,"
"Not until you change my plight,"
Jacob was serious and steadfast
with his request,
Jacob wanted and knew that He had
to receive God's blessing,
Jacob wanted God's best.
This time Jacob wanted to be blessed right,
That was the only way to change his plight,
And so,
Knowing that Jacob was determined and bold,
Knowing that Jacob would not and refused to
let him go,
The Angel gave Jacob his blessing,
The angel asked Jacob,

"What is your name?"
As If not to know,
Then Jacob told him so,
Jacob meant swindler,
Then the Angel blessed Jacob,
The angel erased his former destiny, all sorrow,
Tragic things that were to be,
The angel, He changed His name to Israel,
Which meant a prince indeed you will be,
He took away Jacobs fright,
He changed Jacobs's plight,
And then the angel took his flight,
He did not give up that Jacob,
Until the blessing was bestowed,
Jacob held on and did not let go,
Jacob realized that in order to be blessed
to be steadfast and never to let go,
I wonder do you know what it takes to be blessed?
Especially when you look around and your
 life is quite a mess,
Jesus said,
Behold,
I come quickly,
Come to me everyone and receive,
I give to all gladly everything
You will ever need.
Do not ever give up until you receive your
blessings, your deliverance, and your "Eternal
Salvation"
from Jesus, our Savior,
our Lord and Heavenly King.

From All The Way

From,
All the way from the throne,
And,
From let there be light,
and it was so,
From the Son of God,
To the seed of the woman,
From the seed of Abraham.
Isaac,
And David,
From being born of a virgin and
being called Immanuel,
From the womb to the cradle,
And being born in Bethlehem,
From being called "The Bright And
Morning Star,"
To Savior for All,
To being called out of Egypt,
And being baptized by "The Holy
Spirit,"
While being placed under
water and being baptized by John,
From the Heavens opening up
As the Heavenly Father announced
"This Is My Beloved Son In Whom
I am Well Pleased",
To being a Prophet like Moses
After the order of Melchizedek,
From childhood to Priesthood,

From praying to our Heavenly Father
In Gethsemane Garden,
From public ministry,
To working of miracles
While teaching godly principles
 and parables,
From preaching in the temple,
To being meek, caring, and lowly,
From being compassionate and
without guile,
To being despised by his brethren,
And a stumbling block to the
Pharisees, Seduces,
And being hated and rejected
by the Gentiles and Jews,
And then, being despised by most all,
From being betrayed by a friend,
And the disciples forsaking him,
To being sold for 30 pieces of silver,
From standing before Pilot,
And being smitten on the cheek,
To His visage being marred,
To being spit on and scourged,
And grieved for by His mother,
Mary,
From carrying the cross all the way to
Calvary,
From suffering in silence,
To having feet and hands nailed

by the Romans to the cross while
He bleeds,
From being forsaken by The Heavenly
Father while covered by Sin,
Hanging there in agony with a
Crown of thorns pressed in his head,
While blood ran down his face skin,
From being mocked and given gall
and vinegar for drink instead of water,
When He cried,
"I thirst within",
From garments being parted and lots
cast for his vesture,
From being called a transgressor,
While interceding for murders,
From bones not being broken,
But,

Being pierced in His side,
To hanging on the cross
until He died,
From being buried with
the rich and flesh not
seeing corruption,
To ascending on high,
To His glorious resurrection,
To restoration in Glory,
And sitting on the right hand of God,
To forever now Savior, Lord and King,
The universal God of all,
From the cradle to the cross,
From the grave to eternal praise,
Jesus Christ!
Lord, God, Savior of the world,
Lord, God, Savior of all!

Alive

As I watch the dawn of the day,
As the night stars depart,
As the moon skedaddles,
And the morning, glorious sun displays
Its' bright beams,
I am blessed,

Alive, safe,
Being counted in a vast number
Of those allowed by the almighty God,
To behold a brand new day,
Praise be to Jesus,
Praise for this another glorious day!

God's Will

God's will is pure,
God's will is sanctification,
God's will is eternal life,
God's will is lovely,
God's will is for his Holy Spirit to

Guide you day and night,
God's will is a guiding light,
God's will is found in his word,
The will of God will bless you,
It will bless your life just right.

Prayer And Meditation

Prayer and meditation,
 Is communication between
You, Jesus and God The Father,
How this takes place,
Where this takes place,
When this takes place,
Is not the matter,
Some folks pray louder
than others,
Some folks pray real soft,
For some,
It is when they get a break to
meditate,
Some folks pray along in a
group with all others,
Some pray with prayer tapes
and music,
For many,
It is a combination of it all,
It is not a male or female way,
It is communication between
God worshipers and their Lord,
Just simply pray to God,
Our prayers when daily prayed,
Should have adoration, supplication,
contrition and thanksgiving, worship
and praise,
There are emergency prayers that Jesus,
God hears,
We send these with whatever words comes
out as we pray,
Jesus gives attention to our words,
He listens intently to what you say,
Jesus left the example of
The Our Father Prayer,

Some folk's prayers are silent
meditations between them and
their God,
It is time spent in worship,
That only Jesus, God and the
prayer experiences alone,
Samuel's mom petitioned such
meditations,
While Solomon called down fire that
fell from above,
The king turned over and petitioned
His request of years straight to God,
While Daniels petitions were daily, and
sprung forth out of devotion and love,
David's prayers were of warrior, praise,
protest and request,
Then Jesus in the garden's prayers were
ade in solid meditation and anguish for
Our eternal future,
For our,
Strength to with jubilation finish the battle,
Courage for us to pass our tests,
Endurance, faithfulness and wisdom,
for us,
To be kept knowing that the tests that were
before us we would have to endure,
Perseverance and strength all the way
through,
 To complete our assignments, task,
Ministry and ministering,
For it is our Godly mission to carry
Christ's Cross until the very last,
Until we are like Paul,
Like Christ,
Finished.

ABC Poem

All must come to understand inherited Salvation blessings

Being aware of your redeemed privileges for it is essential

Coming into this knowledge will change your present situations

Do whatever it takes to keep constant prayer times

Everything you trusted in before Jesus abandon

Failing to receive Salvation and trust Jesus will leave you doomed

God gave us an inheritance through Jesus so claim yours

Having Jesus die for us gave us inherited eternal blessings

Indescribable mercy, Salvation and provision is now yours

Just accept these facts and walk in the blessing, favor from God

Keep following God by obeying his word and praying to Jesus

Live your life by God's written word and the Holy Spirit's guidance

Many have tried to make their own way to heaven in vain

Only to need Jesus to show them the correct and righteous way

Praying has saved lives from many a dire circumstance, and hell

Quiet time with Jesus is quite rewarding and comforting as well

Remember to always pray, read your bible and obey God's word

Salvation will always be free and available to all who will receive

Turn your heart towards God, towards Jesus and away from all sin

Under Jesus protection you are covered with sure blessings

Value your soul as does Jesus and God the Father

Will you give your heart to Jesus today?

Xtra time to live is not promised unless you make heaven the goal

You need to come to Jesus now, abandon sin for a righteous crown

Zero in on eternal life and join in with those reigning forever.

GOD WILL CHOOSE

No need to worry or fret about any matters,
God will choose how He will answer,
He knows how to bless and straighten
out your mess,
He has in mind for you His very best,
He will you deliver from enemies who
deem their selves as resourceful and clever,
Crushing those who exalt themselves high
above the heavens,
God sits on His throne,
God sends blessings,
Deliverance,
Answers,
Needed care,
And God does send judgment as well on
 many matters,
God sent Moses,
Samuel,
and
Elijah to name just a few,

To carry out deliverances and deliver messages
On behalf of His people,
On behalf of you,
And, yes, Jesus to die for all and this includes you,
You must become a servant like Joseph,
Daniel,
Job,
Abraham,
Martha,
Mary,
And Paul,
Prophets and dedicated servants from the Bible,
Servants like the faithful servants of God today who
worship and walk only the Jesus way.
Have faith and believe that God can do anything,
And then you will experience the most amazing
Answers,
Deliverances,
Blessings!

HAVE YOU ANY LOSSES

Have you any losses?
Have you had dreams deferred?
Have there been disappointments?
Have there been blessings ripped
away, shattered?
Missed opportunities,
Or,
Brick walls and obstacles,
Prayers seemingly unanswered,
Sickness that appears to not go anywhere,
A magnitude of problems that insists on
staying there,
Just will not disappear,
 Go away,
Well,
I have your now answer,
Your counterclaim,
Today there is a word,
Your faith has prevailed,
This is your moment,
Your petitions have been heard,
Your supplications and prayers,
The devour is rebuked,
The enemy is a liar,
His time has expired,
The angels have commenced victorious
warfare on your behalf,
Your towering enemies are now falling
down,
They have exalted themselves above the very God
Of creation,
This is what their master Satan did,
They are carrying his violence against
you and God again as Jesus has said,
But the "Blood Of Jesus",
Is the power and all the victory you will
Ever need,

Just plead it,
They have to scatter,
They are defeated,
They have been crushed by the "Cross" and torn to
shreds,
Jesus Christ is making anointed visitations of
Comfort and defending victory,
You have been selected to be blessed
and too be delivered from among the crowd,
For when you choose Jesus,
His love chooses you and flows down,
To cover you from all sins,
The blood of Jesus beckons Jesus deliverance,
The blood, the blood,
Nothing but the blood of Jesus,
Sometimes our nights are long winded,
With what seems like no help that totally delivers,
us from our circumstances,
It seems to trickle moments of favor and not
the complete deliverance,
Afterward followed your frustration,
You get wore out and your vision spiritually
is not there or blurred,
Now there is disappointment and despair,
Prophecy after prophecies but no true or
lasting deliverance from far or near,
That season is over,
Your offerings are honored,
Your worship has been blessed,
Prepare now for your deliverance,
The way has been prepared,
Now stand in agreement with these anointed words,
God's true, anointed deliverance, God's favor,
Rest on all these spoken words,
Now may the grace of God be with you in Jesus name,
Amen.

Do You know That I Forgive You

I really do not understand
how I can,
Or why,
Immeasurable hurt abounded inside after you,
This thing, these things you did,
I was perplexed, confused and
wondered why,
Because hurt may come when people
make mistakes,
But when done on purpose,
Many a soul inside dies,
Depression,
Rejection,
Insecurity,
Distress,
Languish,
And gloom,
I knew I had to find myself
In a forgiving state,
Or my life would be over soon,
Could I find the strength to forgive
Pass all the hurt,
Pandemonium,
Turmoil,
Self blame and even shame,
My groaning enlightened my senses
And allowed me to refute every
self accusation of blame,
But, I forgive you,
My feelings swayed like leaves blown
By a strong wind,
Back and forth,
Sometimes fiercely and other times violent,
Wanting revenge as I cried,
Sobbed,
Inconsolable whimpers,
Inner being left hollow,
Then miraculously,
My emotions,
They finally subsided,
Allowing a shimmer of healing inside,

I lamented,
I started listening to a minister,
Forgiveness is what is constantly ministered,
Well, when you are hurting,
Truly wounded,
Pounded by the offense, offenses,
Memories hurling you to the abyss,
Nothing said like forgiveness most times matters,
In fact,
You would rather die,
But ,
Inside I did, I continued to die,
My soul inside continued to die,
I realized that I had to let this go,
This one thing I now understand and realize,
That is,
Bring all and every situation to God who
Already knows,
And ask him to help you to heal and forgive,
Jesus will handle the situations and comfort your
Soul,
So,
My advice to you is live,
Let it go,
Let Jesus carry the hurt,
Take care of restoration,
Take care of justification,
Grant you a resurrection and
manifestation of acceptance and love,
Bless you,
Give you peace and nourish your soul.
And if you are the offender,
Stop,
To Jesus you bow your knees,
Ask for forgiveness please,
And those who you are offending,
Attacking,
Hurting,
Let them go,
The freedom you give them is the same
freedom that will save your own soul.

KATAUTA

Calvary
Calvary is where
I stood guilty needing Jesus
Blood to cleanse me clean.

The Cross

At the cross Jesus
Died and gave his life for mine
And now I am set free.

CARPE DIEM
Being A Blessing

"That sun just came blasting through the blueness of sky like a brand new pair of shiny shoes sparkling on display!" What a burst of energy. You know, how wonderful to start each brand new day with a burst of bright sunshine. Each dewy new morning is a pleasant fresh experience given to you to make whatever your heart and mind set to accomplish before it is done. Yes there are some challenges left over from yesterday but yesterday is now antiquated and tomorrow is filled with expectations of better. "Love God!" Humble your attitude. Search for ones to help or at least someone to uplift and when you have accomplish this for them, reach out for the next one in need of your generosity the most indeed. We can help those who really do not need us but that is not helping. "That is just having something do. So, "Live to love and give each day!" Take advantage of really living by giving and making a difference until you are reaching out your hands to Jesus and then now He will fill it with more than you can ever imagine!

AFFIRMATION

The Bible
I read my bible in my room,
When I awake in the morning,
I read it for guidance, comfort
and wisdom,
I say my prayers in my room,
When the morning comes, eve
time or noon,
I pray for guidance

I pray for comfort,
I pray for wisdom and mercy so that I will
not be consumed,
I worship as I pray no matter the time of day,
I read my bible
I pray,
I worship,
Because I love Jesus with each second I live and
Breath I'll ever take.

Upside Down Salvation/ Sonnet
PETER

Born again, blood washed saint, Jesus ruling within,
Upside down, no glory of man, hissing from the crowd,
Satan marked your life, are you really born again,
Peter, born again, landed on the cross, upside down,
Persecuted, rejected, disrespected, scorned,
Strife, stress, intended humiliation, setup,
Are you ready for this in front of all, life wrecked, torn,
No, you did not mess up, strategic set up, stuck,

Peter understood, He stretched out his arms on a cross,
Are your arms stretched or full, upside down salvation,
Are you a nailed vessel for Jesus, seeking the lost?
Are your wants upside down, steered, no
contemplation,
It will cost your all, crucified world desires,
Jesus cries loud again, crucify flesh, just die.

Kyrielle
BELIEVE GOD

I have learned to believe, trust God,
Instead of panic, I praise, love,
Instead of wondering, I'll pray,
I have learned to believe, obey,

When my health is failing, I trust,
When my marriage is a mess, bust,

When the plots and blocks, swell, assail,
Gods word will always win, prevail,

When friends are gone and say so long,
When accusations are loud, wrong,
When it is hard to love, be strong,
I have learned to believe, trust God,

MONO
HOLY SPIRIT BECKONS

God's Holy Spirit Implores,
He says of me there is so much more,
Come and stay in my presence, adore,
Do not be too lazy, do not me ignore,
What you are to receive, I bare, bore,
When I knock, heed, open the door,
I bring revelations of Jesus, God, for,
With Jesus you must have a good rapport,

Do not be at a distance from me anymore,
With my spirit I will beckon you, I will draw,
I call the young, I call the old, the rich and poor,
I beckon every human with life from shore to shore,
Your relationship with God I will restore,
I will grant your heavenly language, it's yours,
Seek, pray, worship, trust, obey, spiritual blessings
galore.

Christ In The Poem
Do You Know Jesus

Do you know Jesus? King Jesus,
You should! He is a mighty friend,
He will cleanse you from all your sins,
&******&
To know Jesus is to love him, Adore and worship him,
All day long as much as possible I dance, sing praise hymns,
When circumstances are a horrid, Jesus changes them,
He will love you, Help and favor you, Guide, Remove all grim,
&*****&
Value his presence, be moral,
He'll waste demons, without toil,
Obey his commands, stay loyal,
&*********&
Jesus sends His Spirit,
Holy Spirit, You inherit,
Not based on merit,
&******&
Do you know Jesus?
You have to, You must,
He died for all, us.

Mirror Sestet Heaven Awaits

Throne of God dwells in heaven for it is the golden realm,
And there also are our luminous homes,
Homes for Saints of God, Saved by Christ blood alone,
Alone on the cross Jesus died for all our sins, He left His throne,
Heaven is a place of rest for all worry souls and yet we are all chosen to be there, no one is excluded so heed to God's beckons,
Beckons and pleas Jesus sends to each heart every second,
because Jesus does not want you to miss out on,
Being and dwelling forever in his presence in heaven,
You should not ignore this and then depart the earthly realm,
Because then in heaven with Jesus you may not eternally dwell,
Dwell with Jesus each and every day here as well, talk to him,
Give him your heart and attitude, He wants to send His forgiveness and salvation plan directly to and for you.

Bauk
MISTAKE

He should have known,
Now I moan, toss,
And groan, sleep lost,
Much did cost mistake,

Now crossed, grieved, sad,
Jesus plead, pled guilty,
Much dread, need Jesus,

Sestina
THE BLESSER

The blessed has come to bless everyone, us, all,
The wise did ride under the bright star shining down,
He came in fragile, the star showed where He arrived,
The star gleamed in the dark, bright, night sky,
twirling, rays,
He laid enthroned on hay, He brought joy, salvation,
The sky lit gloriously with jubilation,

Many times woes and doom ensconce jubilation,
Twisting perils, Soaring, thundering trials, crush
most all,
Down from His glory with power, and salvation,
Jesus thrusted, pulverized evil, casted it down,
That beaming star was on assignment, a swords ray,
The ray star would demolish foe forces arrived,

The star was shaped like sword to conquer foes arrived,
A purpose of safe keeping, glad jubilation,
Pungent, vile troops cringed at Jesus power force rays,
Jesus power rays demolished, ruined evil, all,
Traveling over terrain, the wise kings kneeled down,
They worshiped our redeeming king of salvation,

He left his robe, put on flesh for our salvation,
Though affliction, persecution, temptation He arrived,

There's no evil force that will prevail, it's crushed
down,
All trials, tribulations, brings jubilation,
Because they brought from heaven Jesus, God, angels,
them all,
Pick up your sword, and fight with Jesus power rays,

When you pray the Holy Spirit sends power rays,
To infuse you with strength and power, salvation,
No weapon formed prospers, annihilate foes, all
Jesus came with deliverance, He has arrived,
Jesus reigns and rules, Conquer with jubilation,
You may suffer, sob, and fall but do not stay down,

Endurance is your sure victory, don't be down,
Healing was given through salvation, power rays,
Call upon Jesus with love and jubilation,
He announced our sanctification, salvation,
He gave power once the "Holy Spirit" arrived,
Now everyone, no matter where can serve him, all,

The blessed came down and blessed everyone,
blessed all,
His holy power rays heals sickness bringing jubilation,
Jesus, the blessed, brought salvation, He arrived!

PANTOUM
GOD'S WORD

As I read God's word,
I meditate on the scriptures,
God's comforts soothes heart,
I pray in meditation,

I meditate on the scripture,
I lay before him listening,

I pray in meditation,
Jesus gives a message vision,

I lay before him listening,
God's comfort soothes heart,
Jesus gives a message vision,
As I read God's word,

Kryielle
PLEAS

O Lord our God who hears our pleas,
Who grants heed, as we bow to thee,
We come before thy mercy seat,
With fervent, urgent, painful needs,
Father God, Jesus save us please,

We are thy servants, meek, loyal,
Grant gracious relief, from sorrow,
My soul cries from a shattered heart,
Let sympathy for me not part,
Father God, Jesus save us please,

Mockery, feindishness, hear me,
These are the plots, schemes,
meanness, theme,

I am counted among redeemed,
I endeavor to live righteously,
Father God, Jesus save us please,

And yet my cross I not regret,
I carry gladly though I may fret,
All the way to heaven, I pray,
Until you give my crown that day,
Father God, Jesus saves us please,

Eternal comfort, joy, instead,
Of shame, abominations, dread,
Every tear wiped by your jewel hands,
Gleaming with power and command,
Father God, Jesus loved, saved me.

AUBADE
GLORIOUS

Glorious! Glorious! Is the bright new dawning day,
She strolls in gorgeously, with the rays of the sun,
Beaming down on the vegetation and greenery,
All wet from the dewy mist covering its yielded leaflets,
She then touches the sky with light that's blossoming
a pure crystal blue in total glorious view,

Glorious! Glorious! Is the blessed new day dawning,
Blessed by God, Its creator, as it strolls across the sky
above the lands, oceans, ponds, and seas,
Welcoming windows its light begins to appear in,
As it awakens the sleepy heads, breathing in God's
oxygen.

I Am Afraid Of REPENTANCE

I am afraid of more people dying without hope,
I am afraid of more people dying without faith,
I am afraid that people will treat each other more unkind,
I am afraid that insensitivity to people's needs will
reach an all-time high,
I am even afraid that disasters from nature will be on
the increase, and that this will create poverty,

I am afraid of more perils, horrors, terrors,
I am afraid of dismal tomorrows,
I am afraid that insanity will continue to escalate,
I am afraid that the earth from corner to corner will
sound with wailings of anguish, tear streaming cries,
failing hearts, and devastated lives,
I am even afraid that there will be no remedy or cure
for the many diseases that scientist will yet be
perplexed by, symptoms of some being extremely
painful, sore,

I want nothing more than peace, real solutions,
I want joy, not wrath, or wailing, or hearts downcast,
I want genuine love, kindness, care, perpetuated
everywhere,
I want I forgive you and will you please forgive me a
natural way of flowing sincerely without regret or
dismay, or an underlying scheme,
I even want folks no longer to be afraid to live where

they desire, without crime, or threat of any neighbor,
any government, or people who in their community
reside,

I want all human kind to truly repent from their hearts
and not just let admitting wrong doings be a mere
thought practiced in their mind,
I want all to know that Jesus died for all mankind and
that
God loves them so much until it cannot be
contained in
our humanly created minds or thoughts of any kind,
I want all to know and realize that God created
everyone,
I want them to understand that this world is
God's world and that He created it and owns
everything in it including all humans born, each
and everyone, that means He is in charge of the living
and the dying,
And I want all to repent truly of their violent behavior,
wicked sins, rebellion and disregard, lack of God, Jesus
Holy Spirit reigning within, and living without God's
favor,
Most of all I want all to believe in hell and heaven
because one or the other of them is where you'll be and
dwell in at the end,
until your eternal end.

JESUS THE NAVIGATOR

Jesus will navigate you through,
Life's difficulties,
Pains,
Sorrows,
Shame,
Defeats,
Disgrace,
Losses,
Tribulations,
Unpredictable, unseen, complicated circumstances,
All ruins,
And defame,
The I think I'll never be the same again,
However,
Jesus also navigates us through all things wonderful,
grand, and good,
The pleasant,
Happy,
Joyful,
Elevation,
Promotion,
Favor,
Fame,
Glorification,
Bountiful blessings,
Everlasting Life,
Salvation,
Eternal Life,
All things down from heaven sent,
Jesus is the navigator of all if you let him in,
If you let this be,
For Jesus will never force himself on anyone,
He is quite the gentleman,
He is the best manager of all of life's circumstances
whether good or bad,
He is the blessed navigator into a blessed
forever at your end,
Your forever "Savior,"
Guide,
Keeper,
The blessed navigator of life,
Your eternal friend.

BE BLESSED

Be blessed
Because you were blessed to wake up
this morning,
To see God's awesome, brand new day,
Be blessed,
Because you are blessed to see the bright
new sun rays beaming across your bed,
Across a sunlit room,
You are full of life,
You are blessed,
There is a bright blue sky and green,
glowing grass,
God created the perfect nature scenery,
Beautiful and vast,
Be blessed as you open your bible,
As God's word by you is being studied and read,
Be blessed as you praise God with your hands
lifted up above your head,
In jubilation and in praise,
From all you have within,
For when you draw near unto Jesus,
He will saturate your praise and tears with his
anointing,
And then He will bless your worship because your
voice of praise
Is what He longs and yearns for and loves daily too
hear and respond too,
Be blessed to be a blessing,
Sharing with all what God has allowed you
to give and share,
For this is what beckons your blessings to come
from far and near,
Be blessed in all you do,
In all you accomplish,

May God the Holy Father, Jesus His Son
bless and prosper you,
With spiritual blessings which brings earthly
blessings and favor
Too,
May you be blessed with wisdom,
All your needs,
Purpose,
Favor,
Friendship,
And Godly influence,
Be blessed with prosperity,
Comfort,
Healing,
Peace,
Acceptance,
Most of all Love,
Be blessed with faith, patience, courage, and
encouragement,
May the beatitudes rule your life,
Be blessed with Eternal Life,
The Salvation from the cross,
Be blessed from the top of your head to
the bottom of your toes,
May you always be a blessing wherever
you may dwell or go,
Just Be blessed!
"The Lord bless you
and keep you;
the Lord make his face shine on you
and be gracious to you;
the Lord turn his face toward you
and give you peace."
Numbers 6:24-26 | NIV

The Commanded Praise

God, our Heavenly Father left us the "10
Commandments",
He commanded us to follow them,
If we do as commanded, there will be much
reward and from God the Father and praise,
God commanded praise from that He created, made,
He commanded that we lift our hearts and minds
each day in worship, sacrifice, just heart rendering
Praises,
God from the very beginning commanded the "Light"
to give him glory and praise,
He commanded the light with its glorious, glowing,
brightening, beaming forces to ablaze the earth with
its sun's shimmering sparkles,
And so then the light illuminated the earth with its
glorious array of brightness and beaming sunlight
sparkles,
Then the sparkles put on a glowing, illuminating,
sparkle show
Of praise from the sky to the earth beautifully
projecting
light picture scenery everywhere,
The scenery was so clear and translucent beautiful like
diamonds reflecting upon all water surfaces,
Then God commanded the darkness to glorify him,
And so the darkness gave way to the light,
And then the darkness kept an illustrious, regal, velvet
appearance
for the night time where the stars, moon, and celestial
creations could reside and they do abide there,
Then God spoke to the waters and commanded they
they glorify him with diversity,
And so the waters divided into oceans, streams, ponds,
seas,
lakes, rivers, and water falls,
With mighty wave power shows from the oceans by
swaying back and forth with powerful waves,
And twinkling sparkles of moving water under
sunlight
from the ponds that also sparkled as they passed over
rocks
from lakes into streams and beyond,
Also with just a glorious steady flow as it descended
over water falls,
Then God commanded the earth to praise him,
And so vegetation begin to appear, and grow,
Trees of every sort,
Animals of every kind on foot,
Flying insects and birds of every kind filled the air,
Every flower of every kind and shrub appeared,
Every bush and all living things great, small, gigantic,
tall,
And then the water accompanied with sea animals
great, enormous, wide and small,
Then the skies said "We will not be left out either,
No not at all,
So then dew, rain, midst, and clouds,
And the clouds twirled and made picture shows that
Made God's Heart fill with joy and the entire heavenly
host cheer,
All creation including man Said "We are here",
And All creation together bowed down and praised
God The Holy Father's name,
And God Smiled,
His heart was overjoyed,
And God said that this is good,
And still today,
All The Heavenly Father wants is your praise.

Psalm 150 New International Version (NIV)

Psalm 150

[1] Praise the LORD.[a]

Praise God in his sanctuary;

praise him in his mighty heavens.

[2] Praise him for his acts of power;

praise him for his surpassing greatness.

[3] Praise him with the sounding of the trumpet,

praise him with the harp and lyre,

[4] praise him with timbrel and dancing,

praise him with the strings and pipe,

[5] praise him with the clash of cymbals,

praise him with resounding cymbals.

[6] Let everything that has breath praise the LORD.

Praise the LORD.

Rewards For Inner Love

To you,
You are so considerate,
You are truly patient and kind,
What great folks are made of,
Your style,

Your encouragement,
Your friendship,
Thanks for everything all the time,
You are one of the best!

SONGS
COMPOSER
AUTHOR THELMA CUNNINGHAM

SONGS: COMPOSER: Thelma C. Cunningham
Melodies: Thelma C. Cunningham
Note: God Given Talent : Composed:
Both Melody and Written Lyrics.
Time Arrangements
Song Tittles

HALFWAY SALVATION

Twice
God ain't got no halfway salvation......
God ain't never done anything without a purpose in mind,
He saved my soul,
And filled me completely with the Holy Ghost,
He didn't halfway do it and He was right on time,
Let me say it again,

God ain't got no halfway salvation......
God ain't never done anything without a purpose in mind,
He saved my soul,
And filled me completely with the Holy Ghost,
He didn't halfway do it and He was right on time,

I was traveling and doing my own thing,
I wasn't thinking about heaven or some Holy King,
I was smoking, drinking, and doing whatever I pleased,
Then one day Jesus knocked me down off my plateau to my knees,

He said" What do you think you are doing?"
"Don't you know you gotta answer to me,
You can die and go to hell or stop your sinning and learn how to serve me,

I'm the lord Jesus,
I am that Holy King,
I will save your soul and in heaven with me you will be,
I say,
God ain't got no halfway salvation......
God ain't never done anything without a purpose in mind,
He saved my soul,
And filled me completely with the Holy Ghost,
He didn't halfway do it and He was right on time,

I say,
God ain't got,
No halfway salvation,
God ain't got,
No sinners in heaven
No sinners in heaven,
He will save you,
He will save you,
He will save you real good,
Save you real good,
Cause God ain't go no,
God ain't got no halfway salvation.

SAVE THE CHILDREN

Save the children..........
Everybody gotta help to,
Save the children,
Save the children..........
Everybody gotta help to,
Save the children,

Do you know that the world has truly changed,
Do you know that this is not a safe and friendly place
to live,
People are dying,
The children are crying,
Cause there is no mom or dad to be found,

Save the children..........
Everybody got to help to,
Save the children,
Save the children..........
Everybody got to help to,

Save the children,
Do you know that you can give yourself, your time,
your funds,
Your protection if nothing else,
You can be their leader,
Someone they can look up too,
Dry their tears fill their tummies,
Give a coat, a pair of shoes,
Send some money, and some clothes,
But for sure this I know,
All can do this, Say a prayer.

Save the children..........
Everybody got to help to,
Save the children,
Save the children..........
Everybody got to help to,
Save the children.

NOTHING IN THIS WORLD LAST FOREVER

Nothing in this world last forever,
Not the moon not the stars,
Not the sun, not today,
Not even tomorrow any oh way,

Nothing in this world last forever,
Not the moon not the stars,
Not the sun, not today,
Not even tomorrow any oh way,

I think I'll serve Jesus,
He's the only one with the forever plan,
And it's eternal salvation for all mankind across the
land,

This is the only way,
You got to live for Jesus, and you got to live this
every day,
And the way of the cross, it is the way of the lamb,
Do you want to live?
Do you want to live?
Do you want to live?
Do you want to live?

Live again,
Do you want to live with the forever Son?
Forever dream,
Forever Peace,
Forever life,
Tell me,
Do you want to live with Jesus Christ in His eternal
reign?

Nothing in this world last forever,
Not the moon not the stars,
Not the sun, not today,
Not even tomorrow any oh way,

Nothing in this world last forever,
Not the moon not the stars,
Not the sun, not today,
Not even tomorrow any oh way,

I think I'll serve Jesus,
He's the only one with the forever plan,
And it's eternal salvation for all mankind across the
land.

ISN'T IT SOMETHING

MUSIC INTRO
Isn't it something, oh isn't it something,
When life don't turnout the way you thought it would,
Isn't it a heartbreak, so, much of a heartbreak when you
Plan things but they don't turnout the way you
thought it would,

Jesus has all the solutions to all heartaches not
understood,
He is the comfort that you need,
For all the upside downs and I thought it would,
He's the only answer you'll ever need,
"MUSIC"
Isn't it something, oh isn't it something,
When life don't turnout the way you thought it would,
Isn't it a heartbreak, so, much of a heartbreak when you
Plan things but they don't turnout the way you
thought it would,
On Calvary, Jesus died for every sin and sinner,

All broken hearts, all streaming tears and all your fears,
And why because our Father God ever loves and cares,
Now isn't it something to know that Jesus loves you so,
And now those heartaches must vacate, they must go,

Jesus grants His loving healing to anyone who upon
him calls,
It does not matter, the pain, the stress, the struggles, he
has the cure,

They all must go,
Because of Jesus,
Oh yes, because of Jesus,
Because my Jesus loves you so,

Because of Jesus,
Oh yes, because of Jesus,
Because my Jesus loves you so,

OH PRAISE THE LORD

"Oh praise the lord", 1st soprano
"Oh praise the lord", 2nd soprano
"Oh praise the lord", Alto
"Oh praise the lord", Tenor
All
"Oh praise the lord",
"Oh praise the lord", "Oh praise the lord,

"Oh praise the lord", 1st soprano

"Oh praise the lord", 2nd soprano
"Oh praise the lord", Alto
"Oh praise the lord", Tenor
All
"Oh praise the lord",
"Oh praise the lord", "Oh praise the lord,
"Let all heaven and earth together praise the lord,
Recitation

Psalm 33 King James Version (KJV)

33 Rejoice in the LORD, O ye righteous: for praise is comely for the upright.

2 Praise the LORD with harp: sing unto him with the psaltery and an instrument of ten strings.

3 Sing unto him a new song; play skillfully with a loud noise.

4 For the word of the LORD is right; and all his works are done in truth.

5 He loves righteousness and judgment: the earth is full of the goodness of the LORD.

6 By the word of the LORD were the heavens made; and all the host of them by the breath of his mouth.

7 He gathers the waters of the sea together as a heap: he lays up the depth in storehouses.

8 Let all the earth fear the LORD: let all the inhabitants of the world stand in awe of him.

9 For he spoke, and it was done; he commanded, and it stood fast.

"WE Glorify-same way as beginning

Magnify

Soprano:

Oh hallelujah, oh hallelujah, oh hallelujah, oh hallelujah, oh hallelujah,

Oh praise the Lord,

Same time Alto:

We glorify, we magnify, we praise Jesus our King.

All:

Oh hallelujah, oh hallelujah, oh hallelujah, oh hallelujah, oh hallelujah,

Oh praise the Lord,

WE HAVE COME

All
"We have come before the Lord to praise his precious
holy name,
And nothing is going to block his praise,
"We have come before the Lord to praise his precious
holy name,
And nothing is going to block his praise,
"We have come before the Lord to praise his precious
holy name,
And nothing is going to block his praise,
Solo
Yes, Well,
When I woke up this morning,
God's sun was beaming,
Everything was beautiful and everything was okay,

Just the way my Heavenly Father created things,
So when I look arounds to behold God's glorious story
of creation,
I lift my hands and voice and I cannot help but praise
his name,

"That's why I've come to praise his name.
All
Twice
"We have come before the Lord to praise his precious
holy name,
And nothing is going to block his praise,
"We have come before the Lord to praise his precious
holy name,
And nothing is going to block his praise,
"We have come before the Lord to praise his precious
holy name,
And nothing is going to block his praise,
Solo adlib
I've come to praise,
I've come to praise,
Because he's so good to me,
He is such a great God,
Pure and Holy,
So I've come to praise….

I WAS JUST A SINNER

"I was just a sinner who was living every day,
Who had no reason to think that I really needed
a God,
"I was just a sinner who was living every day,
Who had no reason to think that I really needed
a God,
MUSIC
But then one day my life started spinning out of control,
And I cried Jesus,
Save me,
I need you right now to come and rescue me,
I might surely die, If you do not save me,

I don't know who you are,

But I know who I was,
I was so lost and sad, And I really needed help,

But then one day thank God,
I bent my knees and prayed,
"And I cried Jesus, Save Me",
Give me brand new life,
Lord Jesus you are my Savior and king,
You are my Savior,
You are my Savior,
You are my sweet peace,
Your my salvation,'
Thank you for rescuing me,
You are my Savior, Lord God Almighty King.

FALLING

Falling,
Falling,
Falling,
Falling,
Seems like hopelessly falling, falling,
Falling,
Falling,
Falling, Falling down,
 Seems like hopelessly falling, falling,
Falling,
Falling,
Falling,
Falling,
Seems like hopelessly falling, falling,
Falling,
Falling,
Falling down,
 Seems like hopelessly falling,
Falling,

There were time when I thought that I was strong,
But without the help of Jesus I have no strength of
my own,
Facing this world with its troubles and its woes,
Nowhere to turn to I thought,
And nowhere to go,
This left me,
Falling,
Falling, Falling down,
Seems like hopelessly falling,
Falling,
Falling,
Falling, Falling down,

Seems like hopelessly falling,
Falling,
Now I know Jesus is my strength, my hope, and peace,
He is my friend and in him I have no needs,
I am so saved from myself and the fear of dread and
defeat,
For I have Jesus who is the only answer to stop me
from,
Falling,
Falling,
Falling, Falling,
Seems like hopelessly falling,
Falling,
I found that Jesus Christ will stop those tumbling
troubles,
Over throws, upsets and woes that are,
Falling,
Falling,
Falling, Falling, Falling,
Seems like troubles sometimes knock me down,
They leave me,
Falling,
Falling,
Falling, Falling, Falling,
But then Jesus comes and rescues my soul,
From the tumbling down,
He stops me from,
Falling,
Falling,
Falling, Falling, Falling,
Jesus rescues me from hopelessly,
Falling,
Falling.

LOVE EVERY

Love every moment,
Love all your sisters and your brothers,
And love the creator,
For God He gave you everything,
And, He made you all you are,
And all you can do in return is love each other,

Love every moment,
Love every moment,
Love all your sisters and your brothers,
And love the creator,
For God He gave you everything,
And, He made you all you are,
And all you can do in return is love each other,

I use to love only for a moment,
Only for when I felt the love,
Flowing through my mind and through my heart,
But now I know not to let it depart,
Because my God who made me,
He made me to love forever,

Love every moment,

Love all your sisters and your brothers,
And love the creator,
For God He gave you everything,
And, He made you all you are,
And all you can do in return is love each other,

I love every moment,
I love my life and all I do,
I love my God and even you,
I love my Savior,

I love every moment and I love the truth,
I love my salvation and the freedom of being
brand new,
For my Jesus Christ is love and his love is for everybody
Including you,

Love every moment,
Love all your sisters and your brothers,
And love the creator,
For God He gave you everything,
And, He made you all you are,
And all you can do in return is love each other,

I'VE LEARNED

I've learned to wait on God,
I've learned to trust his word,
I've learned not to force my will into the circumstance,

I've learned that God, God will do, Just what he
decides is
the will and the solution to the situations,
All my life I always was use to having my will and
my way,
That got me nothing but trouble and a hard course to
being humble,

If you know like I know, You will gladly come to Jesus,
And you won't wait and be as foolish as I was,

I've learned to say yes to God,
I've learned to obey his voice,
I've learned to obey what is written in his word, In his
word,

I've learned to do his will, cause I'm no longer foolish,
stubborn, and
Stumbling,

If you are wise you will stop all your sinning,
Get on God's side because it's the only team that's
winning,
Now I am all about loving and obeying God,
Because I've learned to trust in Jesus.
ablib
Well I've learned,
Yes I've learned,
I've learned so much in life,
But best of al now I am learning all that I need to
know from Christ
Because I've Learned,
You have to learn to that your soul and mind have to
be renewed….

There's No One For Me
My All And All

There's no one for me, to rely on but Jesus,
There's no one for me, to rely on but the Lord,
There's no one for me, to rely on but Jesus,

He's my Lord, He's my all and all,

There's no one for me, to rely on but Jesus,
There's no one for me, to rely on but the Lord,
There's no one for me, to rely on but Jesus,

He's my Lord, He's my all and all,

He's my Lord, He's my all and all,
He's my Lord, He's my all and all,

Yesterday I only depended on myself,
Cause I thought that I needed no one else,
But then Jesus came and saved my soul,
And now I know He's my all and all,

There's no one for me, to rely on but Jesus,
There's no one for me, to rely on but the Lord,
There's no one for me, to rely on but Jesus,

He's my Lord, He's my all and all,

If you think that you can make it on your own,
You may suddenly find yourself alone,
If you do I have a suggestion or two,
First find Jesus, then let him save your soul,

There's no one for me, to rely on but Jesus,
There's no one for me, to rely on but the Lord,
There's no one for me, to rely on but Jesus,

He's my Lord, He's my all and all,

Because He saved my soul,
Because He saved my soul,
That's what he'll do for you,
That's what he'll do for you,
That's what he's done for me,
That's what he's done for me,
He's my God, He's Jesus our salvation King,
He is the Lord of everything,
He's my God, He's Jesus our salvation King,
He is the Lord of everything,
He's my Lord, He's my all and all.
He's my Lord, He's my all and all.

IT TOOK A LOVING GOD

I had messed up my life,
I was so, so lost,
I could not even see a tomorrow,
Then somehow Jesus, you came,
and changed things for me,
Because I was so, so worry,

It took a loving God, to reach me,
Caused I could not be touched,
It took a patient God,
To come and change my life,

I t took a loving God, to come and
change the story ending,
The story ending to my life,
I was lost and confused,
I did not know what to do,

I did not know to pray but then one day,
Jesus saved my soul and now I know to pray

and serve him every day,

I had messed up my life,
I was so, so lost,
I could not even see a tomorrow,
Then somehow Jesus, you came,
and changed things for me,
Because I was so, so worry,

It took a loving God, to reach me,
Caused I could not be touched,
It took a patient God,
To come and change my life,

I'm so glad for a loving God,
I'm so glad for a patient God,
Aren't you glad for a loving God,
Aren't you glad for a patient God.
A God who will change the story ending,
The story ending to your life.

DO YOU HEAR ME LORD

Do you hear me Lord,
Do you hear me Lord,
Will you stop to hear me Lord,

Do you hear me Jesus,
Do you hear me Father God,
Will you stop to hear me cry,
Will you stop for me right now,
me cry,
Will you stop for me right now,

I need you right now, right now
Jesus, right now Jesus,
I need you because I'm ready
to listen Lord,
I'm ready to listen Jesus,
Cause I really need you now,
And I 'am calling out Jesus,
Jesus, Jesus,
Jesus,
Jesus, Jesus,
Jesus, Jesus,
Jesus, Jesus, Jesus, Lord,

Do you want me Lord,

Do you want me Lord,
Do you want me Lord right now,
Because I'm ready Jesus,
Take all of me,
Take everything that's not pleasing,
I don't want no sins any more,
I don't want them at all,
Jesus take all on me, I don't want
no one else but you,
I no longer depend on myself,
I depend on you for it all,
Jesus, Jesus,
Jesus,
Jesus, Jesus,
Jesus, Jesus,
Jesus, Jesus, Jesus, Lord,
Do you hear me Jesus,
Do you hear me Father God,
Will you stop to hear me cry,
Will you stop for me right now.

THE LOVE OF THE FATHER

And it's all about the love of the "Father,
Yes it's all about the love of God,
And it's all about the love of the "Father,
Yes it's all about the love of God,

When you're through with you,
When you don't know what to do,
You'll find it's all about the love of God,

And it's all about the love of the "Father,
Yes it's all about the love of God,
And it's all about the love of the "Father,
Yes it's all about the love of God,

When you're through with you,
When you don't know what to do,
You'll find it's all about the love of God,

Through life we have to find our way, the way,
In life we live from day to day,

And nothing will be right,
And nothing will stay right,
Nothing happens without God,
To your heavenly "Father you
should always pray,
Start every morning like this anyway,
It's all about his love to guide and protect,

Do this and he will always send his best
because it's all about the love of God.

And it's all about the love of the "Father,
Yes it's all about the love of God,
And it's all about the love of the "Father,
Yes it's all about the love of God,

When you're through with you,
When you don't know what to do,
You'll find it's all about the love of God,

WHERE WERE YOU

Where were you,
When you heard "Father God" calling your name,
Where were you,
When in the "Book Of Life" He wrote down your
Name,
Where were you,
When you stopped harboring the deep depths of sin,
Did you ask Jesus to come and save you, And take
away
All sin,
Where were you,
When you heard "Father God" calling your name,
Where were you,
When in the "Book Of Life" He wrote down your
Name,
Where were you,
When you stopped harboring the deep depths of sin,
Did you ask Jesus to come and save you, And take
away
All sin,

Did you raise your hands,
Did you say the repentance prayer,
Oh bow your knees with hands raised up in the air,
Did you feel the power of being born again,
Did you feel renewed and knew that all had changed,
And now know that new life had begun,

Right now, Right here,
If you haven't my friend,
You too can be saved,
You can be born again,
Saved and free,
Get rid of misery,
Call on Jesus name and be born again,

Where were you,
When you heard "Father God" calling your name,
Where were you,
When in the "Book Of Life" He wrote down your
Name,
Where were you,
When you stopped harboring the deep depths of sin,
Did you ask Jesus to come and save you, And take
away
All sin,

Because He died for you,
Because He died my friend,
Because He died for you to be born again,
Because He died for you,
Because He died my friend,
Because He died for you to be born again,
He wanted you to be born again.

BLESSINGS SENT

The Lord,
He sends His blessings,
Sends His favor on His people,
We must turn to His will and His way,

Because there is blessings and favor for every day.

The Lord,
He sends His power,
Sends His power on His people,
We must turn to His will and His way,

Because there is power and favor for every day.

The Lord,
He sends His mercy,
Sends His mercy to His people,
We must turn to His will and His way,

Because there is mercy and favor for every day.

Because there is blessings, power, and mercy for every day,
Because there is blessings, power, and mercy for every day.

I FOUND THAT

Music Intro
I have found that,
The only thing that,
I really needed to do was to accept you in my heart,
I have found that,
The only thing that,
I really needed to do was to accept you in my heart,

If I want to live a better life,
I need to accept you in my heart,
Lord I know that I should understand,

That your plans for my life are what you command,
Please help me Jesus,
Save my soul and have mercy on me,

I have found that,
The only thing that,
I really needed to do was to accept you in my heart,
I have found that,
The only thing that,

I really needed to do was to accept you in my heart,

I have decided no more running from you Christ,
Take my life and all my strife,
Lord now I know and completely understand,

If you need me here I am,
I follow all of your commands,
I find myself in love with you, my God here I am,

I have found that,
The only thing that,
I really needed to do was to accept you in my heart,
I have found that,
The only thing that,
I really needed to do was to accept you in my heart,

If I want to live a better life,
I need to accept you in my heart,
Lord I know that I should understand.

IT TAKES OVER

There's a feeling that I get,
When I praise the Lord,
It takes all over my mind,
My body,
My soul,
There's a feeling that I get,
When I praise the Lord,
It takes all over my mind,
My body,
My soul,

All over my mind, my body and soul,
Praise the Lord,

There's a power that sets me free,
There's a power that sets me free,
It takes all over my mind,
My body,

My soul,
It takes all over my mind,
My body,
My soul,
There's a power that sets me free,
It is the power of Jesus Christ my Lord,
Well it's the power of Christ our Lord,
It takes all over my mind,
My body,
My soul,
It takes all over my mind,
My body,
My soul,
There's a feeling that I get,
When I praise the Lord,
It takes all over my mind,
My body,
My soul.

I CAME TO PRAISE HIM

I came to praise him,
I came to praise him,
I came to praise him,
I came to praise him,
God has been so good to me,
Uooooh uo uo,
I came to serve him,
I came to serve him,
I came to serve him,
I came to serve him,

God has been so good to me,
Uooooh uo uo,
I came to serve him.
I came to worship,
I came to worship,
I came to worship,
I came to worship,
God has been so good to me,
Uooooh uo uo,
I came to worship.

232

WE BROUGHT OUR PRAISE

We have come into the house of the Lord and when we
Came we brought our praise,
We have come into the house of the Lord and when we
Came we brought our praise,
We have come into the house of the Lord and when we
Came we brought our praise,
So have come into the house of the Lord and when we
Came we brought our praise,
Yes have come into the house of the Lord and when we
Came we brought our praise,
We have come into the house of the Lord and when we
Came we brought our praise,
So let us shout and mangnify him,
Yes let us stand and lift up our praises,
So let us shout and mangnify him,
Yes let us stand and lift up our praises,
So let us shout and mangnify him,
Yes let us stand and lift up our praises,
For we have come into the house of the Lord and
when we
Came we brought our praise.

SAVE ME JESUS

Save me Jesus, sop
Save me Lord, alto
Save me Jesus, sop
Oh save me Lord, alto
Save my heart and soul right now, all
Save me Jesus, sop
Save me Lord, alto
Save me Jesus, sop
Oh save me Lord, alto
Save my heart and soul right now, all

You are my God and my deliver, SOLO
You set me free from all sin and shame,
Without you my life will end in eternal damnation,
So please, save me Jesus, with your cleansing blood,
Save me Jesus, Save me right now,
Save me Jesus, sop

Save me Lord, alto
Save me Jesus, sop
Oh save me Lord, alto
Save my heart and soul right now, all
Save me Jesus, sop
SOLO
Save me Jesus,
Please save my soul,
Deliver me from myself cause I need you this I know,
Have mercy Jesus,
Have mercy now,
Come be my Savior, Come be my Lord,
Save me Jesus, sop
Save me Lord, alto
Save me Jesus, sop
Oh save me Lord, alto
Save my heart and soul right now, all

ALL I WANT

I will send my son and let him die for you,
All I want is your eternal happiness and peace,
I will let him die on a cross with suffering,
All I want is your love for me,

I will let him bleed until you are free,
All I want for you is salvation,
I will allow him on the cross to cry out to me,
Just so you can reign eternally with me,
Music
Come and live with me for your eternity,
I ask you this please as my son dies and bleeds,
Such a price to pay for your eternal reign,
But I would do it again, Just to have you here in
heaven,

I am God your Father and Jesus is my son,
We rule and reign from the righteous throne above,
One day soon you will reign with me,
Your heavenly Father, Jesus your savior and my Son,

And all the angels and heavenly host that be,
I am God your Father and Jesus is my son,
We rule and reign from the heavenly throne above,

Music
Come and live with me for your eternity,
I ask you this please as my son dies and bleeds,
Such a price to pay for your eternal reign,
But I would do it again, Just to have you here in
heaven,

I will send my son and let him die for you,
All I want is your eternal happiness and peace,
I will let him die on a cross with suffering,
All I want is your love for me,

I will let him bleed until you are free,
All I want for you is salvation,
I will allow him on the cross to cry out to me,
Just so you can reign eternally with me,

DO YOU FEEL REALLY GOOD

Do you feel really good when you come to praise the
Lord,
Do you feel really good when you come to praise his
name,
Do feel really good when you clap and stomp your feet,
Do it make you feel good when Jesus name you praise
and plead,

Do you feel really good knowing that salvation is free,
Do you feel really good about your life and eternity,
Music
Jesus is the way, the truth and the light,
He will rescue you both day and night,

Come serve a holy King and King Jesus is his name,
He will set you free and you will live eternally,
Come change your life around and then you'll feel real
Good like me,

Music
Jesus is the way, the truth and the light,
He will rescue you both day and night,

Come serve a holy King and King Jesus is his name,
He will set you free and you will live eternally,
Come change your life around and then you'll feel real
Good like me.

TO SERVE JESUS

I only want to serve Jesus,
I only want to serve God,
I only want to love Jesus from my heart,
All, my everything belongs to him,

I only want to live righteous,
I only want read my bible and pray,
I only want to witness about Jesus name,
This is the only thing that matters to me,

One day Jesus is coming back for his saints
To dwell with him forever,

We will worship at his throne,
All the time and forever,
Just praising his name,

Singing hallelujah Amen,
Singing hallelujah Amen,

Singing hallelujah Amen,
Singing hallelujah Amen,
And,
I love, I love, I love, I love Jesus,
I praise, I praise his name,
God is everywhere,
He will meet you there,
I love adore and praise his name,
I love adore and praise his name,

I only want to serve Jesus,
I only want to serve God,
I only want to love Jesus from my heart,
All, my everything belongs to him,

I only want to live righteous,
I only want read my bible and pray,
I only want to witness about Jesus name,
This is the only thing that matters to me,

DOWN AND OUT

If you should see, e,e, me,
Down,
Down and out, ou, out,
Tell me what, would you do,
Would mistreat me,
Or somehow me talk about,
If you,
One day run into me and I'm down and out,
Would you mistreat me,
And the only you do for me, is me talk about,
If you should see, e,e, me,
Down,
Down and out, ou, out,
Tell me what, would you do,
Would you mistreat me,
And somehow me talk about,
If you ou,
One day run into me and I'm down and out,
Would you mistreat me,
And the only you do for me is me talk about,

You see, Sometimes people start out,
There just doing great,
Everything is okay,
God's good all the time,
Yes He is,
But one day,
They might just fall down, down and out,

And if you see them,
Oh,

What would you day,
What would you do,
If you should see them and they are down and out,

Tell me what would you do, ohou,
Would you have compassion or would you just them
Talk about,
So if you should ever, ever see me,

In my down, In my down and out,
Would you have some compassion,
Or would you me,
Would you me talk about,

You see,
Sometime this life,
It just isn't fair, isn't right,
No matter what you do, or how you fight,
Piople just want to pull you down and take your life,
And if it wasn't for Jesus,
Their cruel ending would be your only plight,
The down and out,

And then this would take good people
and God to change those things,
To make it better,
What it should be,
Just right,
If you should see, e,e, me,
Down,
Down and out, ou, out,
Tell me what, would you do,
Would mistreat me,
Or somehow me talk about,
If you,
One day run into me and I'm down and out,
Would you mistreat me,
And the only you do for me, is me talk about,
If you should see, e,e, me,
Down,
Down and out, ou, out,
Tell me what, would you do,
Would you mistreat me,
And somehow me talk about,
If you ou,
One day run into me and I'm down and out,
Would you mistreat me,
And the only you do for me is me talk about,

LISTING 2 CATEGORY "WELL I'M STILL PRAISING MY GOD'S NAME'

Music Intro
Well I'm still praising my God's name,
Well I'm still praising my God's name,
Well I'm still praising my God's name,
Well I'm still praising my God's name,
Though the enemy surrounds me and tries
to block my every path,
Still I'm still praising my God's name,
Still I'm still praising my God's name,
Well I'm still praising my God's name,
Well I'm still praising my God's name,
Well I'm still praising my God's name,
Well I'm still praising my God's name,
Though the enemy surrounds me and tries to
block my every path,
Still I'm still praising my God's name,
Still I'm still praising my God's name,

But I'm still praising my God's name,
Yes I'm still praising my God's name,

Solo
"Jesus come and rescue me,
Save my soul from the enemy,
Shut them down on this side,
Shut them down on all sides,
I plead the blood of Jesus both day and night,

"The word of God says your blood
was shed just for me,

Call on Jesus,
1st Peter:19 says,
19 but with the precious blood of Christ,
a lamb without blemish or defect.
KJV
1st Colassians:14
14 In whom we have redemption through
his blood, even the forgiveness of sins:

John 17:2-23
KJV
2 As thou hast given him power over all flesh, that
he should give eternal life to as many as thou hast
given him.
3 And this is life eternal, that they might know thee
the only true God, and Jesus Christ, whom thou hast
sent.
Lord Jesus deliver me,
Save my soul from the enemy,
I'm pleading your blood and serving faithfully,
I'm still praising your holy name.
Well I'm still praising my God's name,
Well I'm still praising my God's name,
Well I'm still praising my God's name,
Well I'm still praising my God's name,
Though the enemy surrounds me and tries to
block my every path,
Still I'm still praising my God's name,
Still I'm still praising my God's name.

I JUST GOT SAVED

I just got saved,
I just got saved,
I just got saved,
By Jesus,
It's a serious matter,
I just got saved,
I just got saved,
I just got saved by Jesus,
The only begotten Son,

I just got saved,
I just got saved,
I just got saved,
By Jesus,
It's a serious matter,

I just got saved,

I just got saved,
I just got saved,
Through though and by Jesus blood,
And I'm on my way to heaven,

I just got saved,
I just got saved,
I just got saved,
By Jesus,
And now born again and happy,

I just got saved,
I just got saved,
I just got saved,
By Jesus,
By God's only begooten son.

WORSHIP GOD

I......worship God,
I worship God right now,
I......worship God,
I worship God right now,

I......worship,
I worship God right now,
I......worship God,
I worship God right now,

I......worship,
I worship God,
I worship God right now,

Let's come together,
Let's praise his holy name,

I......worship,
I worship God,
I worship God right now,

I......worship,

I worship God,
I worship God right now,

Worship God with all your heart and soul,
Just love him with all your mind,
Tell the Lord how much you really, really love him,
Worship God with all your heart,
Worship God with all your mind,
Just worship God with all your heart, mind and soul,
Just worship God with all your heart,
Just worship God with all your heart,
Just worship God with all your mind, heart and soul.
I......worship,
I worship God right now,
I......worship God,
I worship God right now,
I......worship,
I worship God,
I worship God right now,

Lets come together,
Lets praise his holy name.

THE BLOOD OF JESUS

When the blood of Jesus was streaming down when
He was
Dying on Calvary it covered everyone,
And that means you and me,
When the blood of Jesus was streaming down when
He was
Dying on Calvary it covered everyone,
And that means you and me,
When the blood of Jesus was streaming down when
He was
Dying on Calvary it covered everyone,
And that means you and me,
When the blood of Jesus was streaming down when
He was
Dying on Calvary it covered everyone,
And that means you and me,
'The blood of Jesus covers everyone.......
It covered everyone,
'The blood of Jesus covers everyone.......
It covered everyone,
The blood of Jesus will cleanse you from all sin,
The blood of Jesus will cleanse you from all sin,
The blood of Jesus will give you power from within,
The blood of Jesus will give you power from within,

It's the blood of Jesus,
The blood of Jesus will wash you cleanse you,
 save your soul and make
You whole and bold,
It's the blood of Jesus,
It's the blood of Jesus,
Come on under the blood........
Come, Come,
Come on under the blood.........
Oh come,
Come, come,
Just come on under the blood........
Come on under the blood,
Come,
Come on under the blood,
The blood of Jesus cleanses everyone........
The blood of Jesus cleanses everyone,
And the blood of Jesus is for everyone,
The blood is for everyone,
And the love of Jesus is for everyone,
The love of Jesus,
The blood of Jesus,
Is for everyone.

NEW JERUSALEM

My God's getting us ready to go,
To New Jerusalem,
My God's getting us ready to go,
To New Jerusalem,
My God's getting us ready to go,
To New Jerusalem,
My God's getting us ready to go,
To New Jerusalem,
One day we will go
Go oooo

Go oooo
Marching in,
Marching in,
To the New Jerus….alem, rusalem,
One day we will go
Go oooo
Marching in,
Marching in,
To the New Jerus….alem, rusalem,
One day we will go marching in to the New Jerusalem,

Play your tambourines,
Sing and shout,
Wear you dancing, shouting shoes,
Steady your crown,
As you move about,

The Lord Jesus is coming with a shout,
Are you ready to go home?
The Lord Jesus is coming with a shout,
Are you ready to go home?
My God's getting us ready to go,
To New Jerusalem,

My God's getting us ready to go,
To New Jerusalem,
My God's getting us ready to go,
To New Jerusalem,
My God's getting us ready to go,
To New Jerusalem,

Play your tambourines,
Sing and shout,
Wear you dancing, shouting shoes,
Steady your crown,
As you move about,

The Lord Jesus is coming with a shout,
Are you ready to go home?

The Lord Jesus is coming with a shout,
Are you ready to go home?

LEAVE THEM BEHIND

Leave them with God,
Leave them with God,
On the way to receiving salvation leave those sins
under the blood,

Leave them with God,
Leave them with God,
On the way to receiving salvation leave those sins
under the blood,

Jesus loves me this I know,
For the bible tells me so,
All his people here below,
They are cleansed by his precious blood,

Leave them with God,
Leave them with God,
On the way to receiving salvation leave those sins
under the blood,

Leave them with God,
Leave them with God,
On the way to receiving salvation leave those sins
under the blood,

COME FOLLOW JESUS

Hey, you over there,
Come follow Jesus,
Come follow Jesus,
Come follow Jesus,
Come follow God,

Hey, you over there,
Come follow Jesus,
Come follow Jesus,
Come follow Jesus,
Come follow God,

You aren't doing anything with your life,
You're just going around in circles,
All you have been doing is fussing and fighting,
Doing anything but what's right,
If you expect to go with Jesus when He comes,
You will need to receive salvation,
So bend your knees and repent and stop sinning,
With the help of God's Holy Spirit.

Hey, you over there,
Come follow Jesus,
Come follow Jesus,
Come follow Jesus,
Come follow God,

Hey, you over there,
Come follow Jesus,
Come follow Jesus,
Come follow Jesus,
Come follow God,

Somebody help him please,
Somebody help him,
Somebody help him,
Somebody help him please,
Somebody help him,
Somebody help him,
Somebody help him please,
Somebody help him,
Somebody help him,
Somebody help him please………………

"Boom!"
Epilogue
6th Act
Now he is gone,
He is gone,

Now He is gone,
He,
He is gone,
He is gone, Gone to His God!"

Thinking About It-song

You have been talking, and you have been saying,
It is always simpler cause you escape while playing,
You promise so much, and you act on time,
You see so little, that is yours and mine,
When faced with facts, your words you deny,
(2) Just what's really what's going on with your heart
inside,

But baby when I am close to you and there is
No one else to hold but me but you,
I feel what surges through your heart and mine,
It's just like breath in your body as we breathe,

So I have been thinking about you,
And I have been wondering too,
Just what I am I to do with this emotional Cruise,
Between me and you, Since we have been up and
down,
Heads spinning all around, But when I reach for you,
And when you need me too,

"Do I stop and tell my mind that you want to be here
all the time,
Or do I keep reality and ignore the words you that say
to me,
Or do I watch what you only display on any given day,

Or do I just trust and believe what happens when we
just breathe,

We just breathe,
We just breathe,
We just breathe….yea…..
Nice and easy……yea…..

Breathe,………
When we just breathe……yea
I'll just breathe………..
You have been talking, You have been saying,
It is always simpler while you escape through playing,
You promise so much, you act on time,
You see so little, of what is yours and mine,
Has all simply faded with time, tell me what to do,
Cause I am asking you,
Do I just breathe……
Do I just breathe…..
This emotional Cruise….
Am I really still in love or
Is it changes that I am simply going
Through,
Do I just breathe,…..
What am I to do…….

2 version but first

282

Thinking About It-song

You have been talking, You have been saying,
It is always simpler while cause you escape through
playing,
You promise so much, You act on time,
You see so little, that is yours and mine,
When faced with facts, your words you deny,
Just what's really goin on in your heart Inside,

But baby when I am close to you and there is
No one else to hold but me,
I feel what surges through your heart and mine .
Just like breath in your body as you breathe,
So I have been thinking about you,
And I have been wondering too,
Just What I am I to do with this
Emotional Cruise,
We have been up and
And when you need me too,
We just breathe, down,
Heads spinning all around,
But when I reach for you,

We just breathe,
We just breathe yea
Nice and easy yea
"Do I stop and tell my mind
That you want to be here all the
Time,"

Or do I keep reality and ignore
The words you that say to me,
And watch what you only display,
On any given day
Or do I just trust and believe,
What happens when we just
Breathe,
When we just breathe,yea
I'll just breathe,
You have been talking,
You have been saying,
It is always simpler while
You escape through playing,
You promise so much,
You act on time,
You see so little,
What is yours and mine,
Has all simply faded with time,
Tell me what to do,
Cause I am asking you,
Do I just breathe,
Do I just breathe,
This emotional Cruise,
Am I really still in love or
Is it changes that I am simply going
Through,
Do I just breathe,
What am I to do,

YOU SAID WHAT YOU SAID

Song

4 times Intro
I remember what you said to me,
When you said what you said to me,
I remember,

1st
I heard you say it nice and clear,
I understood you perfectly,
Now there is nothing left but silence all around,
As I try to lift my face up off the ground,

2nd
How can you be so dark and cold
After all the love that we shared,
Was I not the one honest and true,
After all, our love was strong and bold,

I 'm all alone in the crowd and I'll admit that I am
traumatized,
As I send my prayers about our love to the father in
the sky,
Baby all I know is that we are through and if just for a
little
While I want to remember you un-cruel,
Walking in and out as if I am nothing and
never really mattered to you,
Is this what I deserve from you?

Does it make any sense to try and love this love again?
Can you find the strength to revive this love again?
Can you my friend, background

Do you think I would be standing here, shivering with
no voice,
if I could find the way by myself without your love on
my own?

I remember what you said to me,
I heard you say it nice and clear,
I understood you perfectly,
Now there is nothing left but silence all around,
As I try to lift my face up off the ground,

Does it make any sense to try and love this love again?
Can you find the strength to revive this love again?

You must be careful what you do, although at times I
know
That I too was guilty of hurting you,
Because when it is cold it gets colder and right now
that is you,
And the crueler gets crueler, and the shrewder more
shrewd,

But just remember one day when you go to say my
name,
It will be with I never met to hurt you,
By the time that you turn around you will realized that
I'm gone,
And that so long that you boldly said now echo's in
your head,

How can you be so dark and cold?
After all the love we shared,
After all, your love was bold,

I remember what you said to me,
I heard you say it nice and clear,
I understood you perfectly,
Now there is nothing left but silence all around,
As I try to lift my face up off the ground,

Does it make any sense to try and love this love again?
Can you find the strength to revive this love again?

Be careful how you love, love wrong because it too is
unforgivable when tossed about and thrown.
But if nothing to know and if nothing else is said,

I remember what you said to me,
I heard you say it nice and clear,
I understood you perfectly,
Now there is nothing left but silence all around,
As I try to lift my face up off the ground,

Mom-Thelma Chapman

HAPPIER TOMORROW

If only I could sing a song, that would bring
About a much happier tomorrow,
It doesn't have to be long,
If only I could sing a song that would bring
About a much happier tomorrow,
It doesn't have to be long,

Well if only I could sing a song,
That would bring about in your heart a much
Happier tomorrow,
It doesn't have to be long,
Just as long as you sing along,

There are just too many fears and tears and folks aren't
getting along,
Got to have a better tomorrow,
Much happier tomorrow,
There is just too much crime, folks during time,
stealing and killing,
Deceiving and dealing,

We need a better tomorrow,
There is just too much willing to be cruel to your
neighbor,
Being lazier and crazier,
I think we need a better tomorrow,
We got to have a better one,

If only I could sing a song that would bring
About a much happier tomorrow,
It doesn't have to be long,
If only I could sing a song that would bring
About a much happier tomorrow,
It doesn't have to be long,

Just as long as it takes the time to ease your mind,
Let's make a better tomorrow,

Stop glorifying violence and sorrow,
If only I could sing that song.

WHY ARE YOU ON YOUR WAY

Why are you on your way?
Without serving,
Without serving,
Serving God,
Why are you on your way?
Without serving,
Without serving,
Serving God,
Don't you know He loves you?
He loves you and needs you to love,
Don't you know He loves you?
Oh, oh He loves you,
Yes He loves you,
He's God,
Why are you on your way?
Without serving,
Without serving,
Serving God,
You got to stop your hating, your drugging, your killing, and repent,

You got to stop your assaulting, all sinning, and serve God,
You got to cherish life, and living, giving, and prayer,
You got to read God's bible, start obeying, and start praising
Jesus,
Start praising God,
Jesus Christ He loves you,
He loves you, He's God,
Why are you on your way?
Without knowing,
Without knowing the Father's love,
Don't you know He loves you?
He loves you and needs you to love,
Don't you know He loves you?
Oh, oh He loves you,
Yes He loves you,
He's God,

JUST PUT YOUR TRUST IN HIM /Tomorrow

Just put your trust in,
The one who understands, your tomorrow,
Just put your trust in,
The one who understands, your tomorrow,
Just put your trust in,
The one who has the plan, for your tomorrow,
Just put your trust in,
The one who has the plan, your tomorrow,
Put your trust in the one who understands tomorrow,
Put your trust in the one who navigates tomorrows,

Many times,
We sit around,
Get around,
Think around,

Plan around,
Tomorrow,
Many times,
We sit around,
Get around,
Think around,
Plan around,
Tomorrow,
Just put your trust in,
The one who understands, your tomorrow,
Just put your trust in,
The one who understands, your tomorrow,
Just put your trust in,
The one who has the plan, for your tomorrow,

Don't you worry about tomorrow because tomorrow
Takes care of tomorrow before tomorrow ever gets
Here,
Don't you worry about tomorrow because tomorrow
Takes care of tomorrow before tomorrow ever gets
Here,
Don't you worry about tomorrow because tomorrow
Takes care of tomorrow before tomorrow ever gets
Here,

Get it out of your head,
Get it out of your head,

Get it out of your head,
Get it out of your head,

Tomorrow will take care of tomorrow before tomorrow ever gets here.

JUSTICE SOUND

There's a sound going around,
That's breaking ground,
It's called the justice sound,
It's moving, it's moving,
There's a sound going around,
That's breaking ground,

It's called the justice sound,
It's moving, it's moving,
There's a righteous cause,
A Godly move,
In spite of you and you,
It's breaking through, it's moving, and it's moving,

Enough is enough,
No more accept injustice,
There's a God above and He's filled with love,
He always been there,
He will always save and deliver,
He will protect, He is the giver,

He is the God of justice,

He is the God of Justice,

TUMULTUOUS STORM

When I'm in a tumultuous storm,
Furious circumstances,
Nothing going right,
Everything going wrong,

When tomorrow is taking too long,

Seems like sunshine is gone,
And way too hard to stay strong,

When you're alarmed and can't stay calm,
Troubles that seem to toss your life around,
And knock your feet off the ground,

I won't sink,
I won't sink,
I will hold to Jesus,
I'll pray to Jesus, I'll trust in God,
God will tell your enemies to be gone,

Jesus loves you and me Jesus cares,
He'll calm all those fears,
Handle all the dread and the tears,
Provide the strength to go in,
Cease the worry and make me strong,

So if you're in a tumultuous storm,
Just hold on,
Nothing going right,
Everything going wrong,

When tomorrow is taking too long,
Just call on Jesus, Call on God,

He's the deliver,
He's the healer,
The protector,
Jesus is God,
He's the deliver,
He's the healer,
The protector,
Jesus is God,

THERE ALL GONE

There all gone, sop
There all gone,
All my sins are gone,
There all gone, alto
There all gone,
All my sins are gone, tener
There all gone,
There all gone,

All my sins are gone,
There all gone,
There all gone,
All my sins are gone, all
Jesus saved my soul, On Calvary,
And His precious blood washed, cleansed and set me free,

Have you been washed by the blood of Jesus,
Have you been cleansed, saved and set free,
Have you received your victory?
Have you received your victory?

We'll He'll be coming back again for you and me.
Jesus saved my soul, On Calvary,

And His precious blood washed, cleansed and set me free,

Have you been washed by the blood of Jesus,
Have you been cleansed, saved and set free,
Have you received your victory?
Have you received your victory?

We'll He'll be coming back again for you and me.

NOT HOPELESS

You're never just hopeless,
Got to do everything all by yourself,
You're never just on your own,
And only you got to figure everything all out,
You're never just hopeless,
Got to do everything all by yourself,
You're never just on your own,
And only you got to figure everything all out,

Don't you worry,
For God's help will be there,
Don't you worry,
For God's help will be there,

You're never just hopeless,
Got to do everything all by yourself,
You're never just on your own,
And only you got to figure everything all out,

You won't have to worry,
You won't have to figure this all out,

For God is in heaven and He will come down
And He will deliver you,
For God is in heaven and He will come down
And He will deliver you,

You're never just hopeless,
Got to do everything all by yourself,
You're never just on your own,
And only you got to figure everything all out,

Don't you worry,
For God's help will be there,
Don't you worry,
For God's help will be there.

MAKE UP YOUR MIND

Sometimes I feel like I just really don't know which
way to go,
No guide to show,
Oh no,
There are times I walk to fast and sometimes,
I feel like I'm walking slow,
It could be so,
It could be so,

I feel a push a pull, and yet, I still can't get through,
There are times when I feel weak and there are times
That I feel real strong,
But it doesn't last long,

I need somebody, someone to come along and
tell me what's going on,
In my life,
In my life,

But then I look to Jesus,
And I tell him all about everything that's not so right,
And I tell him that I just don't have any more energy to
fight,
Oh no, oh no,
But I got to make up my mind,
Cause you got to fight this fight,

There are times I feel like there outa be an answer
to every prayer I pray, right away,
But I found that it doesn't always happen every time I
pray,
It's just not always that way,

It doesn't mean he doesn't care,

Well these feelings sometimes try to determine if I
want
To go on,

Well sometimes all I want to do….is get out of here,
But the one thing that I know for sure and I do not
Question any more,
And that is Jesus died for me….and you

Well if you begin to read and understand the master
plan
Jesus left it here on the earth,
Maybe some of the things you're going through
Your ups and downs and your hurts, and heartaches
Might make sense to you,
But I don't know,
I really don't know, oh no,

Well I know that there's a heaven,
And I'm just as sure there is a hell,
And I just don't think people understand that
They got to know where they want to go….
Before they leave the land,
Oh yea,
You better be ready to go,
Oh yea,
Ask the questions all the time,
Keep searching till you find,
I got to make up my mind,
To be with Jesus all the time.

GOD CHANGED ME

I was down before,
Being sad and ignored,
I thought that my life was worth nothing at all,

I use to be,
Down and sad,
I use to be,
Really, really, mad,
But that's not how it is anymore,

God came and made a difference,
God came and saved my soul,
God came and changed my life, my mind, attitude
and destiny,

I use to be worrisome,

I use to have no direction,
I felt that sadness had no ending,

I use to think so blurry and dreary,
All the time just worries,
But that's not who I am anymore,

Jesus saved my life,
Jesus came and made me happy,
Now I'm on my wat to heaven,
I rest in Jesus where I've found peace,

I rest in Jesus,
I rest in Jesus where I've found peace,
I rest in Jesus,
I rest in Jesus because that's where I found my peace.

HANGING OUT NO MORE

When you start going to church and you don't
hang out,
People want to know why,
They want to know why,
Tell me why,
They want to know why,
Tell me why,

When you stop cursing them out and refuse to be a
loud mouth,
Believe it or not,
They want to know why,
Tell me why,
They say we know you were never shy,
So tell me why,

Well I can tell you that I found Jesus,
I found the answers to the questions of my soul,
I found life, love, and I found hope,
I found God,

I found God,
I found God,
When He came he changed my mind,
Healed my thoughts and replaced my heart,
Cleansed my soul and made me whole,
I tell you that's why,
Yes that's why,
I tell you that's why,
Yes that's why,

So if you need a brighter, better day and want to live
Eternally with God at the end and always,
Then hang out with me and Jesus,
You'll have fun you'll see,

You will want to hang out now with me,
We will hang out with God, and Jesus, and the saints,
You will see,
Having fun with Jesus,
The eternal Savior for all to see.

WHILE YOU'RE WAITING ON THE NEXT THING

While you're waiting on the next thing to happen in your life,
How's about considering The Lord Jesus Christ,
While you're waiting on the next thing to happen in your life,
How's about considering The Lord Jesus Christ,
While you're waiting on the next thing to happen in your life,
How's about considering The Lord Jesus Christ,
He just didn't come to die for no reason,
He shed His precious blood to save you and me,
He hung on Calvary and now we are
Redeemed,
By the precious blood of Jesus Christ our King we are Free
While you're waiting on the next thing to happen in your life,
How's about considering The Lord Jesus Christ,
While you're waiting on the next thing to happen in your life,
How's about considering The Lord Jesus Christ,
While you're waiting on the next thing to happen in your life,
How's about considering The Lord Jesus Christ,

WHERE WERE YOU WHEN I CAME

Where were you,
Where were you,
Tell me where were you,
Tell me where were you,
I came a knocking and nobody answered the door,
Where were you,
Where were you,
 Tell me where were you,
Tell me where were you,
I came a knocking and nobody answered the door,

Will you, Will you,
Will you let me in your heart?
I came a seeking,
But nobody answered at all,
Will you, Will you,
Will you let me in your heart?
I came a seeking,

But nobody answered at all,

Do you, Will you,
Will you let me live there,
I'm Jesus your Savior and I will love you
More and more,

Do you, will you,
Will you let me come there?
I will come and bring Salvation to you,

Do you, Will you,
Accept and love my Jesus,
He's the one, who will bring eternal salvation,
Do you, Will you,
Will you love my Jesus?
He's the one who will bring eternal salvation.

MADE IT TO THE CHURCH

I'm really glad you made it out to church today,
I'm really glad you made it out to church today,
I'm really glad you made it out to church today,
I'm really glad you made it out to church today,

And I give God the praise,
And I give God the praise,

I'm really glad you made it out to church today,
I'm really glad you made it out to church today,
I'm really glad you made it out to church today,
I'm really glad you made it out to church today,

And I give God the praise,
And I give God the praise,

You could have chosen to stayed home,
You could have been somewhere else all alone,
You could have just have not wanted to come,
Because of being sad, blue and glum,
You could have been tired and confused,
So stressed out and without help,

So I give God the praise,
Yes I give God the praise,
I'm really glad you made it out to church today,
I'm really glad you made it out to church today,
I'm really glad you made it out to church today,

I'm really glad you made it out to church today,

And I give God the praise,
And I give God the praise.

CAN I GET A YES

Can I get a yes?
Yes, Yes,
Can I get a yes?
Yes, Yes,
Can I get a yes?
Yes, Yes,

If you know that Jesus has died to set you free,
If you know that Jesus gave his salvation and it's free,
If you know Jesus blood is powerful, precious and
costly,

Just say yes,
Yes, Yes my Lord,
Just say yes,
Yes, Yes my Lord,

If you know without him you would be living in
misery,
If you know that Jesus is the only real source of peace,
If you're thankful that Jesus came to make you pure
and holy,

Just say yes,
Yes, Yes my Lord,
Just say yes,
Yes, Yes my Lord,

Can I get a yes?
Yes, Yes,
Can I get a yes?
Yes, Yes,
Can I get a yes?
Yes, Yes.

THAT SMILE

That smile,
It's the only one for me,
It's the one that sets me free,
Will please just smile for me,
That smile,
It's the only one for me,
It's the one that sets me free,
Will please just smile for me,
No one can smile like you,

That smile has so much history,
If only everybody new would took for you to give such
a wonderful
Gift of your smile,

That smile just does so much for me,
You're the only one, who has that smile,
That smile makes my day happy, my day okay,
It's my blessing every day,
You need a wonderful hurray,
 Cause your smile,

Is the only one for me,

If people only knew the pain it took to make that
smile,
This smile can never be forgotten through eternity,
Jesus himself adored this smile because He knew all
about this life,
And your smile,
Is now with the angels in peace,
In heaven you are always smiling down on me,
That's what helps bring me peace,

That smile,
Our see in heaven again,
Can't wait to see it and hold you then,
So keep on smiling for me,
So keep on smiling for me,
Yes,
Your now,
Smiling with the angels and down on me.

I MISS YOU

I miss you,
I miss you,
Yes I miss you,
Oh how I miss you,
I miss you,
I miss you,
Yes I miss you,
Oh how I miss you,

You were a gentle soul,
You were so very bold,
You were so much that cannot be explained,

So filled with compassion,

So filled with wisdom,
So filled with kindness,
So filled with love,

So I miss you,
I miss you,
Yes I miss you,
Oh how I miss you,

You looked out for me,
Treated me like your daughter,
Defended me like no other,
Yet you were firm and very wise,

Heaven must have opened wide,
Overshadowed you with mercy,
For all the love you had inside,
I know they sent an angel, just to be your guide,
Jesus said do not pick my children
Cause only I know who they are,

I miss you,
I miss you,
Yes I miss you,
Oh how I miss you,
I miss you,
I miss you,
Yes I miss you,
Oh how I miss you,
So filled with compassion,

So filled with wisdom,
So filled with kindness,
So filled with love,

So I miss you,
I miss you,
Yes I miss you,
Oh how I miss you.

I WANT TO GIVE IT TO YOU

I want to give it to you,
I want to give it to you,
Um hum,
I want to give it to you,
I want to give it to you,
Um hum,
Wake me, shake me, turn me around, upside down,
Wake me, shake me, turn me around, upside down,
I want to give it to you,
I want to give it to you,
I want to give it to you,
I want to give it to you,
Um hum,
I want to give it to you,
I want to give it to you, I just want to give it to you,
Um hum,
I want to give it to you,
I want to, um hum, um hum,

Wake me, shake me, bend me, turn me around, upside
down,
Um hum, Um hum,
Talk-RAP
You know,
Sometimes in love,
It's hard to get from point A to point B
Getting to love and making love is not always a smooth
transition,
But ah,

What I want you to do right now is think about the
one you want to give that
Thing to,
And the way you want too,
And just do it,
Wake me, shake me, turn me around, upside down,
I want to do it,
I want to do it to you,
I want to do it to you,
I want to do it to you, um hum,
Ha,
Ha, ha, ha, ha, ha,
Ha, ha, ha, ha, ha,
I want to, I want to, I want to,
To you, um hum,
I want to, I want to, I want to,
To you, um hum,
I want to, I want to, I want to,
To you, um hum,
Baby, oh baby,
I want to do it to you,
Um hum,
And I promise, oh I promise,
It's going to be real good, um hum,
I promise, oh baby I promise, it's going to be real good,
Oh um hum,
I want to, I want to, I want to,
To you, um hum,
I want to, I want to, I want to,
To you, um hum,

NOW HE IS GONE
Dedicated To My Brother In Law
Whose Life Went Far Too Soon
Dramatic Opera Skit And Song
God Give You Rest
IN HIM
JIMMY/JAMES CUNNINGHAM

Composed By His Sister In-law
Author Thelma Cunningham
Married To John David Cunningham
17 years as of May 2017
JOHN IS JIMMY'S BROTHER
Jimmy is also survived by his
2 Sisters
Patty Cunningham and Kathy Cunningham

Prologue

NOW HE IS GONE

Now He is gone, Sop 1st
He is gone, He is gone,
Now He is gone,
He is gone, He is gone,

Now He is gone,
He is gone; He is gone, gone to his God,
Now He is gone,
He is gone; He is gone, gone to his God,

Now He is gone, 2nd Soprano
He is gone; He is gone, gone to his God,
1st soprano
Gone, He is gone, He is gone,
Now He is gone,
Gone,

Now He is gone,
Gone,
He is gone, He is gone,
Gone to His God,
2nd Act
Steps not the same,
Not the same for He is man,
Steps not the same,
Not the same for He is man,

Now when He walks,
He is trying to keep the same,
Now when He walks,
He is trying to keep the same,

2nd and 2
Now He does not see through his vision the way things
Use to be,
Now He does not see through his vision the way things
Use to be,

3rd ACT
His mind is fluttering away,
All that's left is dismal and gray,
His mind is fluttering away,
All that's left is dismal and gray,
All that is best is talking away,
All that is best is talking away,

On the floor he sits to lie,
On the floor he sits to lie,

In his hands is what will take the very last
Words, expressions he will say,
In his hands is what will take the very last
Words, expressions he will say,

All written down, time to go away,
All written down, time to go away,

His mind is fluttering away,
All that's left is dismal and gray,
His mind is fluttering away,
All that's left is dismal and gray,

4th Act 1st soprano
All that's left is dismal and gray,
obligatory
Ha, ha, ha, ha,
Ha, ha, ha, ha, ha,

Ha, ha, ha
Ha, ha, ha,
Ha, ha, ha, ha, ha,
Ha, ha, ha,
Ha, ha, ha,

5th Act
Somebody help him,
Somebody help him,

I YIELD

Jesus,
I yield my all to you,
Jesus,
I yield my all to you,
Jesus,
I yield my all to you,
Jesus,
I yield my all to you,
I yield my all to thee,
I yield my all to thee,
Master,
You came and set me free,
Master,
You came and set me free,
Master,
You came and set me free,
Master,
You came and set me free,
I yield my all to you,
Savior,
Save me completely,
Savior,
Save me completely,
Savior,

Save me completely,
Savior,
Save me completely,
Save me completely Lord,
Master, Savior,
I give my mind, heart, my all to thee,
Master, Savior,
I give my mind, heart, my all to thee,
Master, Savior,
I give my mind, heart, my all to thee,
Master, Savior,
I give my mind, heart, my all to thee,

Jesus,
I yield my all to you,
Jesus,
I yield my all to you,
Jesus,
I yield my all to you,
Jesus,
I yield my all to you,
I yield my all to thee,
I yield my all to thee,

Lord You Live In My Heart

Song

All:
As the day is darning and I behold the sun,
One of your most glorious creations,
In the midst of your vast blue sky above,
I'm reminded just how majestic that you are,
And how awesome the things I behold and see,

Je-sus, you live on high,.. and in my heart,
So with joy to you I praise and sing,
You made us to have you as our Lord, God, Savior and
King…..

And so I gladly tell the world, and everyone I greet…..
Just how wonderful you are to me,
Just how wonderful you are to me,

Je-sus you live on high and in my heart, I'll never
depart….
And so to you with joy I sing, And so to you with joy I
sing,

Soprano: 1st
Your works are wonderful,…. and your creation is
grand and splendid,
And you chose… to let me live another day…
(just to give you praise, just to give you praise, 2nd Sop

Altos:
I am in awe, with all you have done and do for me,
As travel through this earth, I behold daily all your
beings,
That you made to worship you, That you made to
worship you,

Tenors:
Loving, kind and wonderful Savior,
A Savior that they really need.
A Savior that they really need.

All:
Je-sus, you live on high,.. and in my heart,
So with joy to you I praise and sing,
You made us to have you as our Lord, God, Savior and
King…..
And so I gladly tell the world, and everyone I greet…..
Just how wonderful you are to me,
Just how wonderful you are to me,
Je-sus you live on high and in my heart, I'll never
depart….
And so to you with joy I sing, And so to you with joy I
sing,

"AND SO TO YOU WITH JOY WE SING!"

R&B SELECTIONS
COMPOSED AND WRITTEN BY AUTHOR THELMA
CUNNINGHAM
AS WITH ALL HER WRITINGS
COMPOSED BECAUSED OF ANALYIZED
EXPERIENCES
IN OTHER WORDS,
THEY WAY SHE SEES THINGS

IT'S COLD OUTSIDE

OH, OH,
It's cold outside,
It's cold outside,
It's cold,
AWE,
OH, OH,
It's cold outside,
It's cold outside,
It's cold,
AWE,
OH, OH,
It's cold outside,
It's cold outside,
It's cold,
AWE,
Warm,
It's cold outside,
But inside my heart is warm for you,

So when you come,
Bring your loving,
Bring your hugging,
And bring the wine,
AWE,
So when you come,
Bring your loving,
Bring your hugging,
And bring the wine,
AWE,

OH, OH,
It's cold outside,
It's cold outside,
It's cold,
AWE,
So when you come,
Bring your largesses,
And anything that's on your mind,

Now when you come,
I'll give you loving,
I'll give you hugging,
All of my time,
OH, OH,
It's cold outside,
It's cold outside,
It's cold,
AWE,
Now when you come,
I'll treat you special,
Love you whenever,
Because your mine,

OH, OH,
It's cold outside,
It's cold outside,
It's cold,
AWE,
But inside my heart is warm for you.

ONE WAY WITH GOD

There's just one way with God,
There's just one way with God,
There's just one way with God,
There's just one way with God,

There's no 2 ways,
No 3 ways,
No 4 or 5,
So if your thing about coming any other way,
There is no way but one way,
The Lord Jesus Christ, He's the only way.

There's just one way with God,
There's just one way with God,
There's just one way with God,
There's just one way with God,

You can't run,
You can't hide,

You must choose heaven or hell,
You must choose where you will dwell,

So if your thing about coming any other way,
There is no way but one way,
The Lord Jesus Christ, He's the only way.

There's just one way with God,
There's just one way with God,
There's just one way with God,
There's just one way with God,

There's no 2 ways,
No 3 ways,
No 4 or 5,
So if your thing about coming any other way,
There is no way but one way,
The Lord Jesus Christ, He's the only way.

WHAT DO YOU WANNA DO

What do you want to do with your life?
What do you, want to do,
What do you want to do with your life?
What do you, want to do,

What do you want to do with your life?
What do you, want to do,
What do you want to do with your life?

There are so many choices it seems you can choose,
There are so many voices telling you what to do,

What do you, want to do,
What do you want to do with your life?
What do you, want to do,

There are so many choices it seems you can choose,
There are so many voices telling you what to do,

Now you must listen and follow a God devoted path,
This path is filled with his wisdom,
God's understanding and his protective love,

What do you want to do with your life?
What do you, want to do,
What do you want to do with your life?
What do you, want to do,

What do you want to do with your life?
What do you, want to do,
What do you want to do with your life?

TAKES A MINUTE

Takes just a minute just to be saved,
In Jesus name, In Jesus name,
Takes just a minute just to be saved,
In Jesus name, In Jesus name,

It takes just a minute just to proclaim,
Who you are in Jesus name,
In Jesus name,
It takes just a minute just to proclaim,
Who you are in Jesus name,
In Jesus name,

It takes just one minute to be washed and cleansed,
In Jesus name,
In Jesus name,
It takes just one minute to be washed and cleansed,
In Jesus name,
In Jesus name,

You can go far, when you proclaim the word of God
and Jesus name,

You can go far, when you proclaim the word of God
and Jesus name,

Life turns brand new and so do you in Jesus name,
In Jesus name,
Life turns brand new and so do you in Jesus name,
In Jesus name,

Takes just a minute just to be saved,
In Jesus name, In Jesus name,
Takes just a minute just to be saved,
In Jesus name, In Jesus name,

You can go far with who you are,
In Jesus name,
In Jesus name,

Takes just a minute just to be saved,
In Jesus name, In Jesus name,
Takes just a minute just to be saved,
In Jesus name, In Jesus name.

SOUND OF THE SAINTS

That's the sound of the saint's praising the Lord, sop
That's the sound of the saint's praising the Lord, alto
That's the sound of the saint's praising the Lord, sop
That's the sound of the saint's praising the Lord, alto
ALL
They say:
Our God is the mighty God,
Our God is the living God,
Our God is Jesus Christ the Lord,
Our God is the mighty God,
Our God is the living God,
Our God is Jesus Christ the Lord,
Tenors
That's the sound of the Saint's,
Clapping their hands,
Clapping their hands,
Altos
That's the sound of the Saint's,
Stomping their feet,
Stomping their feet,
Sop
That's the sound of the saints shouting and praising the
Lord,

Shouting and praising the Lord,

Solo:
Psalm 150
[1] Praise the LORD.[a]
Praise God in his sanctuary;
 praise him in his mighty heavens.
[2] Praise him for his acts of power;
 praise him for his surpassing greatness.
[3] Praise him with the sounding of the trumpet,
 praise him with the harp and lyre,
[4] praise him with timbrel and dancing,
 praise him with the strings and pipe,
[5] praise him with the clash of cymbals,
 praise him with resounding cymbals.
[6] Let everything that has breath praise the LORD.
ALL
For God is Father God,
And His son Jesus is savior and Lord,
So shout everybody and praise your God,
For God is Father God,
And His son Jesus is savior and Lord,
So shout everybody and praise your God.

THERE IS A SAVIOR

There is a Savior,
His name is Jesus,
He came, He died
And when He did He sat all mankind free,

There is a Savior,
His name is Jesus,
He came, He died
And when He did He sat all mankind free,

I got to tell you that He loves you,
I got to tell you that He'll set you free,
I got to tell you that He loves you,
I got to tell you that He'll set you free,

Jesus loves you; Jesus will set you free,

Jesus loves you; Jesus will set you free,

If you're truly lost, you just need Jesus,
Come and be found,
Come and be loved,
Come and find sweet peace,
Salvation is free,

I got to tell you that He loves you,
I got to tell you that He'll set you free,
I got to tell you that He loves you,
I got to tell you that He'll set you free,

Jesus loves you; Jesus will set you free,
Jesus loves you; Jesus will set you free,

LIST 3
WHAT A WONDERFUL SAVIOR THAT WE SERVE

What a wonderful Savior that we serve,
What a wonderful Savior that we serve,
Jesus is so wonderful,
Just wonderful,
Just so wonderful, wonderful,
What a wonderful Savior that we all serve,

What a loving, devoted Savior that we serve,
What a loving, devoted Savior that we serve,
Jesus is so wonderful,
Just wonderful,
Just so wonderful, wonderful,
What a loving, devoted Savior that we serve,

What a mighty, gracious Savior that we serve,
What a mighty, gracious Savior that we serve,
Jesus is so wonderful,
Just wonderful,
Just so wonderful, wonderful,
What a mighty, gracious Savior that we serve,

What a wonderful Savior that we serve,
What a wonderful Savior that we serve,
Jesus is so wonderful,
Just wonderful,
Just so wonderful, wonderful,
What a wonderful Savior that we all serve.

By HIS AMAZING GRACE

By His amazing grace,
I've come to know Jesus,
And I love Him,
Yes I Do,
By his amazing grace,
I've received my salvation by faith,
I declared this,

I do,
Jesus changed my destiny,
Gave me new hope and peace,
His salvation and eternal piece,
Nothing else do I need but his continued love,

I am now free,

Its amazing grace,
How sweet the sound,
That found me; found me when I was lost,
Its amazing grace,
How sweet the sound,

Now every single day,
I've learned to always pray and worship him,
So should you,
Nothing else is better to do,

Than reading God's word and becoming brand new,
This is what I have chosen to do,

Will you too,

Its amazing grace,
How sweet the sound,
That found me; found me when I was lost,
Its amazing grace,
How sweet the sound,
Its amazing grace,
How sweet the sound,
That found me; found me when I was lost,
Its amazing grace,
How sweet the sound,

CELEBRATION

Let's have a celebration,
Let's have a celebration,
Let's have a celebration,
Let's have a celebration,

We'll have a celebration,
We'll have a celebration,
We'll have a celebration,
We'll have a celebration,

We'll have a celebration, about God's love,

Let's hang some party streamers,
We'll dance in the Holy Spirit,
Clap our hands and shout praise the lord,

Let's hang the Holy banner,
Come together all God's people,
Testify both day and night of God and God's love,

Let's have a celebration,
Let's have a celebration,

Let's have a celebration,
Let's have a celebration,

Let's hang some party streamers,
We'll dance in the Holy Spirit,
Clap our hands and shout praise the lord,

Let's hang the Holy banner,
Come together all God's people,
Testify both day and night of God and God's love,

Come on and celebrate,
Come celebrate our God,
Come on and celebrate,
Come celebrate our God,

He is wonderful,
God is worthy,

Come on and celebrate, celebrate,
Celebrate our God,

I LOVE MY JESUS

Uoooo, INTRO 4
I love my Jesus,
Uooooo,
I love my Jesus,
Uooooo,
I love my Jesus,
Uooooo,
I love my Jesus,
Uooooo,
I love my Jesus,
Uooooo,
I love him now,
Uoooo,
I love him now,

Do you love Jesus?
Uooooo,
Do you love Jesus?
Uooooo,
Do you love Jesus?
Uooooo,

Do you love Jesus?
Uooooo,
Do you love Him now,

Will you serve Jesus,
Uooooo,
Will you serve Jesus?
Uooooo,
Will you serve Jesus?
Uooooo,
Will you serve Jesus?
Uooooo,
Will you love Jesus,
Uooooo,
Do you love Jesus?
Uooooo,
Will you serve Jesus?
Uoooo,
Cause I love my Jesus,
Uoooo,
Cause I love him now.

WHEN YOU MAKE UP YOUR MIND

When you make up your mind that you will follow Jesus,
Jesus will be there every single time,
When you make up your mind that will follow Jesus,
You will find that He has been there all the time,

And though every demon in hell,
Will launch a full scale war,
Jesus will come with his angels from above,
And He will defend, deliver and keep you in His love,
Jesus almighty will come down from above,

Jesus will carry you in His arms,
Protect you from all harm,
Bid your enemies farewell and to be gone,

So when you make up your mind that you will follow
Jesus,

Jesus will be there every single time,
When you make up your mind that will follow Jesus,
You will find that He has been there all the time,

When you come under His precious blood,
The blood of the Lord Jesus, Savior and Christ,
Jesus just hovers over you both day and night,

For you Jesus will fight,
Both day and night,
For on Calvary Jesus changed your eternal plight,

When you make up your mind that you will follow Jesus,
Jesus will be there every single time,
When you make up your mind that will follow Jesus,
You will find that He has been there all the time,

NO ONE COULD TELL ME

No one could tell me what I,
No one could tell me what I,
No one could tell me what I,
No one could tell me what I believe,

No one could tell me,
Cause I refused to know,
No one could tell me,
Cause I refused to know,
No one could tell me,
Cause I refused to know,
No one could tell me,
Cause I refused to know,
No one could tell me,
Cause I refused to know about God,

Nothing could save me,
I said just get away,
Nothing could save me,
Cause I'll serve Him on another day,
No one could save me,
Not right now,
Just get away,

Cause I'm okay,

Then one day,
Something happened to me,
It made me change,
I fell on my knees,

I asked for forgiveness,
And now I pray,

Oh please Lord tell me what to do,
Where to go and what to say,
Jesus helps me to believe in you
Accept your Holy guidance every day,

Now this is what I now say,

I want to tell you,
I,I
I want to tell you,
I,I
I want to tell you,
I love the Lord.

IT"S ALL OVER ME

It's all over me,
It's all over me,
It's all over me,
It's all over me,
It's all over me,
It's all over me,
The power of Jesus Christ,
It's all over me,
The power is falling,
And Jesus name I'm calling,
The saints are falling down under the power of God,
Saints are running here and there,
Some lying on the floor everywhere,
The power of God is falling down,
It's all over me,
It's all over me,
It's all over me,

It's all over me,
The Holy Spirit comes down,
And takes control don't you know,
It moves your being, your head, arms, feet, and legs,
The Holy Spirit will make you run, skip, turn and
Roll around,
It will knock you clean on the ground,
It's all over me,
It's all over me,
It's all over me,
It's all over me,

It's all over me,
It's all over me,
It's all over me,
It's all over me,
The power of God is falling down.